STUDIO SCRIPTS

Series editor: David Self

Working

The Boy with the Transistor Radio *Willy Russell*
Good Prospects *Charlie Stafford*
Strike *Yolanda Casey*
George and Mildred *Johnnie Mortimer and Brian Cooke*
Emmerdale Farm *Douglas Watkinson*

City Life

Lies I, II *Willy Russell*
Uncle Sangi *Tom Hadaway*
Short Back and Sides I, II *Alan Plater*

Communities

Shove Up a Bit *Gavin Blakeney*
Hush-a-Bye, Baby *Gavin Blakeney*
Blind Eye *Gavin Blakeney*
Old Fogey *Julia Jones*
Nuts and Bolts *Julia Jones*

Situation Comedy

The Liver Birds *Carla Lane*
Happy Ever After *John Chapman and Eric Merriman*
Rising Damp *Eric Chappell*
Last of the Summer Wine *Roy Clarke*
Going Straight *Dick Clement and Ian la Frenais*

Situation Comedy

Edited by David Self

STUDIO SCRIPTS

Hutchinson
London Melbourne Sydney Auckland Johannesburg

Hutchinson & Co. (Publishers) Ltd
An imprint of the Hutchinson Publishing Group
24 Highbury Crescent, London N5 1RX

Hutchinson Group (Australia) Pty Ltd
30–32 Cremorne Street, Richmond South, Victoria 3121
PO Box 151, Broadway, New South Wales 2007

Hutchinson Group (NZ) Ltd
32–34 View Road, PO Box 40–086, Glenfield, Auckland 10

Hutchinson Group (SA)(Pty) Ltd
PO Box 337, Bergvlei 2012, South Africa

First published 1980
Selection, Introduction and notes © David Self 1980

Set in VariTyper Century Schoolbook

Printed by The Anchor Press Ltd
and bound by Wm Brendon & Son Ltd
both of Tiptree, Essex

British Cataloguing in Publication Data
Situation comedy. – (Studio scripts; vol. 4).
  1. English drama – 20th century
  I. Self, David   II. Series
  822′.9′1408   PN120.A4

ISBN 0 09 142931 5

Contents

Introduction

This volume illustrates the genre of television comedy which is known as 'situation comedy', a kind of light entertainment which can be typified as relying on a group of recurring characters, familiar locations and rather predictable story-lines. It first became popular in this country in the early 1950s, beginning as radio entertainment and transferring naturally and happily to television, as that medium developed in the late 1950s and 1960s.

One of the first radio comedy shows to keep a single story-line running for thirty minutes had been *Life with the Lyons*, which starred the American comedian Ben Lyon and his real-life wife, Bebe Daniels. However, like its predecessors, it relied on individual jokes and its humour did not arise from character or situations. Another popular radio comedy series of the post-war years, *Take it from here*, was first broadcast in 1948. Written by Frank Muir and Denis Norden, it starred Jimmy Edwards, Dick Bentley and Joy Nichols (who was later replaced by June Whitfield). At first, it too consisted only of topical jokes and sketches but, late in 1953, the writers introduced a genuine situation comedy element in the form of the Glum family. (Twenty-five years later, incidentally, the Glums were to be revived as a television series.) The television critic, Peter Black, has chronicled their development:

In a short while the Glums came to take on an identity of their own and even some spurious depth, and whatever Muir and Norden may have intended, they became a sadly touching *ménage*, trapped by the limitations of their lives and aspirations.

Like the figures on Keats's Grecian urn, for ever would Eth love and Ron not stir. Gradually their part in the show expanded until they took over half the time. This move was regarded at the time as a sign of maturity, an indication that *Take it from here* had come of age; unquestionably it could not have happened without a significant growth in the authors' self-confidence and belief in themselves as something more than comic gag-men.

Listener, 3 December 1970

A year later two other writers, Ray Galton and Alan Simpson, developed the first genuine half-hour situation comedy show on radio, *Hancock's Half-Hour*. Peter Black has analysed its structure:

Hancock's Half-Hour began fairly traditionally. It was usual to have a character for the comedian to play against so they got Sid James. He became a shady character, always stealing lead and promoting dodgy schemes; Bill Kerr, the Australian comedian, played an Australian actor who was always out of work; Hattie Jacques was Hancock's secretary and house-keeper. Kenneth Williams played all the other characters. The house was supposed to be in East Cheam because Galton and - Simpson were tickled by the name. It was part of the marvellous freedom of radio that no attempt was made to be consistent. Hancock was supposed to be an actor, just as Sid James was supposed to be a burglar, but sometimes Hancock was rich, sometimes he was starving, sometimes he was an actor, sometimes an army deserter who had been hiding out in East Cheam for years.

Listener, 17 December 1970

Over the years there was much more consistency, as the Hancock character matured, and there was also a move to greater realism, a realism that was maintained when the series transferred successfully to television.

While situation comedy has remained a popular form of radio comedy, it is on television that it has really flourished. Some critics have ventured to suggest that it is with the BBC that it has reached its greatest heights. Certainly many of the most popular series of the 1960s were on BBC Television. Besides *Hancock*, Galton and Simpson wrote several series of *Steptoe and Son*, which featured the two rag-and-bone men, and was set almost exclusively in their appallingly squalid home and its adjacent junk yard. In 1964 *Steptoe and Son* was regularly being watched by as many as 22 million viewers. Other successful BBC series of this period included *The Rag Trade* (about a group of workers in a clothing workshop) and *Sykes*, a long-running series built around the comedian Eric Sykes.

Later series of this decade included *The Likely Lads*, (set on Tyneside), *Marriage Lines* (a domestic comedy series), *All Gas and Gaiters* (involving a group of comic clergymen) and the infamous *Till Death Us Do Part*, which featured the Cockney Garnett family and especially the bigoted Alf, played by Warren Mitchell. This was a joke which nearly backfired: instead of being regarded as purely an eccentric figure of fun, Alf began to be listened to by some viewers as someone whose pontifications had more than a grain of sense in them.

Situation comedy continued to be popular in the 1970s, and in 1977, the *BBC Handbook* was perhaps justifiably self-congratulatory:

The introduction of two new situation comedy series and the

development and enrichment of others made this a good year for BBC Light Entertainment. The two new ones were *The Good Life* on BBC 1 and *Fawlty Towers* on BBC 2. The latter made most impact on the critics and has already won prizes but the former developed a warmth which quickly made it a favourite with many millions. In *Fawlty Towers*, written by John Cleese and his wife Connie Booth, we saw Basil Fawlty, played by Cleese, and his wife Sybil, desperately trying to run a small country hotel, with Andrew Sachs as the Spanish head-waiter, Manuel.

The Good Life, written by John Esmonde and Bob Larbey, depicted a much more happily married couple, Tom Good and his attractive wife Barbara, played by Richard Briers and Felicity Kendal. They were seen to be struggling to be self-sufficient, away from the rat-race, by growing their own produce and trying to keep pigs and other animals in the garden, often to the great concern of their neighbours played by Penelope Keith and Paul Eddington.

The comic creation of the year, however, undoubtedly remained Ronnie Barker as prisoner Fletcher in *Porridge*. In a second series Dick Clement and Ian la Frenais achieved the same very high standard as in the first, including a particularly funny Christmas Eve edition. Once again the strength of *Porridge* lay not only in the comic writing but in the poignancy of many of the situations, together with masterly supporting performances by Fulton Mackay and Richard Beckinsale and also – in two episodes – by Peter Vaughan and David Jason.

Among comedies of another vintage *Dad's Army* showed fresh inventiveness in a new series and its repeats did as well as ever.

The BBC's Comedy Department has constantly to bear in mind the vital need to provide viewers with programmes that are funny north – as well as south – of the River Trent. The success of *Last of the Summer Wine* in 1974–5 was almost exceeded by that of *I Didn't Know You Cared*, based on some books by Peter Tinniswood which the author himself adapted. This introduced a new family to television and starred Robin

Bailey as Uncle Mort and Liz Smith as Mrs Brandon. Meanwhile, *The Liver Birds* continued strongly, brightened by the
arrival in Liverpool and in the programme of Elizabeth
Estensen as Carol. Her coming gave Carla Lane, as writer, an
opportunity which she exploited to the full in some very funny
scripts.

However, situation comedy has not been the
exclusive preserve of the BBC, as is shown by a survey
published in the Independent Broadcasting Authority's
annual guide, *Television and Radio 1980*:

Situation comedies have been popular with viewers since the
earliest days of ITV when real-life husband and wife teams –
like Evelyn Laye and Frank Lawton in *My Husband and I*
and Barbara Kelly and Bernard Braden in *Rolling Stones* –
competed for laughs in series set against a domestic background.

In fact, comedy based on family life appears to present
writers with an almost inexhaustible supply of situations.
Since 1958, when the nation shared the lives of that cockney
family *The Larkins* starring Peggy Mount and David
Kossoff, ITV has continued to derive comedy from such
series as . . .*And Mother Makes Three* (Wendy Craig), *Bless
This House* (Sidney James and Diana Coupland), *Father,
Dear Father* (Patrick Cargill) and many others based on a
family setting.

With the enormous demands of television for new and
original material, it is no surprise that the writers looked to
other spheres of human activity on which to develop their
ideas. And today there is probably not one theme that has not
already been exploited by a comedy series: the Irish/Jewish
tailoring partnership in *Never Mind the Quality, Feel the
Width* (1967), the conflicts between crew and inspector in *On
The Buses* (1969), the exploits of young RAF recruits in *Get
Some In* (1975) or the antics of medical students in *Doctor in
The House* (1969) were all successful series in their time.

Because the British enjoy laughing at themselves, writers

have often exploited the frailties of the human character and in particular of the underdog who has more than his fair share of misfortune. Back in 1962 Jack Rosenthal and Harry Driver created *Bulldog Breed* in which Donald Churchill played Tom Bowler, an engaging young man with a gift for creating chaos, and in the late sixties Ronnie Corbett was the dithering loser in *No, That's Me Over Here.* More recently David Jason suffered humiliation when confronting just about anybody in a position of authority. There was also Norman Wisdom of course, and perhaps the most endearing loser of all, Tony Hancock, who transferred his unique talents to ITV in the 1960s.

Like the general drama output, comedy often reflects social trends. *Man About the House*, for example, appeared at a time when more and more young people in inner-city areas were becoming flat-dwellers, and bold attempts were made in 1972 to help take the tension out of race relations with such series as *Love Thy Neighbour, The Fosters*, in 1976, took things one stage further by becoming the first situation comedy in which all the main characters were black. Every effort is made to avoid offence in any programme that deals with race or religion and no doubt discussions will continue as to whether negative attitudes can be changed by persuading people to laugh at their prejudices.

The high audiences and degree of appreciation are in themselves an indication of the success of ITV comedy series, as indeed are the cinema feature films which have often resulted from the most popular of them and the number of formats which have been sold abroad; but also of significance are the many characters that have been developed into further series. An early example of the 'spin-off' came in 1960 when *Bootsie and Snudge* followed *The Army Game*'s Bill Fraser and Alfie Bass into civilian life. The highly popular *Please Sir!*, which introduced John Alderton as the young teacher in a tough, London secondary school, eventually gave birth to *The Fenn Street Gang*, a comedy series that followed the lives of the rebellious teenagers after they left school. Yootha Joyce and Brian Murphy as the ill-suited landlords in

Man About the House went on to star in their own series –
George and Mildred – when a financial windfall took them to
fashionable suburbia; and their lodger (played by Richard
O'Sullivan) continued to exploit the character of Robin Tripp
in a new series of *Robin's Nest.*

While ITV relies to a large extent on the talents of such
established artistes as Arthur Lowe, Elaine Stritch, Donald
Sinden and Leonard Rossiter, it is also true that many series
have featured newcomers and it was very sad indeed when
last year we were to learn of the death of one of television's
most promising young artistes, Richard Beckinsale.

Whether viewers prefer the down-to-earth Northern humour
of *Leave it to Charlie* (Granada) or the more sophisticated
verbal wit of a series like *Two's Company* (LWT), one thing is
certain: the struggle for writers to maintain originality,
imagination and a consistently high standard will not
become any easier.

Selecting five scripts from all this output for inclusion
in this collection has not been easy – and not solely
because of the quantity of material to choose from.

Many shows, once shorn of the exuberance of their
stars and of the laughter of a studio audience nudging
the viewer into a similar response, fall rather flat. The
words die on the page.

Others get their laughs by ploys which in the cold
light of morning can seem offensive. Some play on
racialist jokes (despite the good intentions expressed
above), and others derive their 'humour' from
stereotyped misrepresentations of minorities such as
immigrants and homosexuals. A surprising number,
including some transmitted quite early in the evening,
rely heavily on sexual innuendo for their humour. Some
are even more explicit, but more often it is oblique
references to the subject which aim to raise the laughs.
(Students might constructively discuss whether they
like such series and how they feel when viewing them

with, for example, their parents.)

Others have been rejected either because they have very few characters (and may therefore be unsuitable for school or college use), or because the scripts are no more than vehicles for particular star comedians and rely heavily on those stars' mannerisms and gestures for their humour. Consequently, in order to present scripts which will work well in the classroom or drama studio. those offered here are ones which have been written, in the main, for actors and actresses in general rather than for established comedians. It is hoped that a balance has been struck between those which have been memorable on television and those which will read well even if deprived of their visual effects. It is also hoped that, besides giving enjoyment in their own right, these scripts will lead to a greater critical appreciation of situation comedy and the elements of their dialogue and structure.

The Liver Birds

This series is unusual in that it is one of the very few comedy series to be written by a woman and to star women. In the early series, the leading characters were Sandra (played by Nerys Hughes) and Beryl (played by Polly James). Eventually Beryl 'moved away' and Carol (played by Elizabeth Estensen) became Sandra's flat-mate. Set in Liverpool, the original 'situation' was very much that of the two girls and the problems they encountered in sharing a flat and finding (and losing) their various boyfriends. Gradually the situation has been expanded to take in their respective families – the socially pretentious Mrs Hutchinson (played by Mollie Sugden) and the Boswells, an eccentric, rather than 'typical' Liverpool Irish Catholic family. Among the

Boswells are the gin-slurping mother (played by Eileen Kennally), the work-shy father (played by Ray Dunbobbin) and Lucian, Carol's rabbit-keeping brother (played by Michael Angelis).

This episode, the fourth from the 1976 series, shows the writer, Carla Lane, at her deftest with a script that ranges from slapstick farce to moments of touching pathos. Like all situation comedies, it exploits a number of running jokes as the characters behave as we expect them to do. Nevertheless, it is in its own right a self-contained play, with natural and unforced humour, deriving from the characters and their relationships as well as from the situation.

Happy Ever After

If *The Liver Birds* derives much of its comedy from the problems afflicting young people, *Happy Ever After* is in some ways the archetypal situation comedy in that it is a husband and wife who are the central characters and providers of the humour.

The basic 'situation' is that Terry Fletcher (played by Terry Scott) is always over-enthusiastic and over-confident. His wife, June (played by June Whitfield, who was also Eth in the radio version of *The Glums*), deflates his sillier aspirations and his pomposity. Her sympathetic character is preserved by being set against the mother-in-law figure of Aunt Lucy. The Fletchers' grown-up children (whom we occasionally meet in some episodes) have left home, and in this first programme of the 1976 series, June longs to have a child to look after again. Once Terry accepts the idea, his behaviour is charmingly predictable. The domestic situation is here extended to include a welfare officer (so that we may laugh at authority) and the schoolboy the Fletchers foster.

It is interesting to speculate why, although we laugh at almost all the other characters, we rarely laugh at June or the boy. They may have funny lines but these are usually at another character's expense.

Rising Damp

In *Rising Damp*, the 'situation' is that of an 'extended' family; a 'family' of lodgers in the seedy lodging house run by Rigsby (played by Leonard Rossiter). Rigsby is a penny-pinching landlord, forever trying to make a little more out of his long-suffering tenants in their freezing, ill-decorated bed-sitters.

A Yorkshire Television press release sketched in the rest of the background to the third series of the show (transmitted in 1976), from which this script is taken:

The new series sees the welcome return to the fold of the genteel Ruth (played by Frances de la Tour) who, early in the last series, departed with wedding bells on her mind, and the local librarian on her arm.

Alas for Ruth – although happily for Rigsby, who has always seen himself as her knight in shining armour – that romance has turned sour. As she admits to Rigsby: 'I realised I'd made a mistake. There was someone I was trying to forget, but I couldn't.'

Rigsby believes that someone is himself, but in fact, Ruth has never really stopped rooting for the African chieftain's son, Philip.

So now the situation is back to square one. Perhaps the wallpaper at Rigsby's dwellings may have deteriorated to an even deeper shade of yellow, there may be a few more layers of dust, a few more running repairs to be added to the ever-growing list, and Vienna, Rigsby's feline champion of the nocturnal dustbin rangers, may have gained another grey hair or two.

Rigsby, self-styled aristocrat of the flat-letting fraternity, still cannot help poking his nose into the private lives of his lodgers, especially those of the fluttering, fading violet, Ruth. He still fancies his chances there.

But Rigsby's romantic aspirations for the unreachable Ruth have scarcely mellowed his striking personality. He's still as mean, grasping, devious, bigoted and prejudiced as ever ... characteristics which equip him well for the continual bouts of in-fighting which take place with the suave, majestic Philip.

As the above outline shows, the lodging house provides an ideal and convincing setting for a whole variety of situations developing from the interplay of the resident characters: it too is a typical situation comedy.

Last of the Summer Wine

This series, set in South Yorkshire, is rather different in nature to the other scripts. Like *The Liver Birds*, it is a northern comedy but the humour and pace are gentler, there is less reliance on actual jokes and there is far more location filming. Nevertheless there is the same interplay of character, especially between the main trio: Foggy (played by Brian Wilde), Clegg, (played by Peter Sallis) and Compo (played by Bill Owen).

Meeting in the tatty café run by the hen-pecked Sid and his domineering wife, Ivy, these three old-age pensioners plan adventures which usually turn into misadventures due either to Foggy's would-be efficiency failing disastrously or to Compo (who is a kind of old-age hooligan) misbehaving in some way. Just occasionally the culprit is the mild and philosophical Clegg who provides a lugubrious commentary on life.

In this episode, the main characters are off on their annual holidays to Scarborough. The location may be different but the situation is the same: the trio banter with each other but unite against the world. In many ways, they are like a group of schoolboy friends, squabbling among themselves while regarding the rest of the world with a mixture of disrespect, scorn and fear.

Not so much a comedy show as a series of comic plays or films, *Last of the Summer Wine* asks us to laugh with (rather than at) old people and also shows us that they can enjoy themselves. It is also rare in presenting young people as gormless and less clued-up than their elders.

Going Straight

As we have seen in the excerpt from the *BBC Handbook* (see page 10), Dick Clement and Ian la Frenais created a very successful series for the gifted comedian and comic actor, Ronnie Barker. This was called *Porridge* and was set in 'Slade Prison', a dour, northern prison. ('Porridge' is prisoners' slang for a period of imprisonment.) Wisely, when the writers felt that they had exploited the situation as much as they could, Fletcher (the character played by Ronnie Barker) was released on parole and a new series was born, *Going Straight*. This was concerned with his attempts to keep out of trouble once he was out of prison. The first episode showed him on the train, travelling home, and the script included in this volume was the second of this first series.

Also in *Going Straight* is Godber (played by the late Richard Beckinsale) who had been Fletcher's cell-mate and is now boyfriend to Fletcher's daughter.

Once again, there is a firmly defined situation, capable of exploitation for several episodes; subtle interplay of established characters and (especially in this script) some highly witty yet natural dialogue – dialogue which was beautifully realized by the original cast but which stands in its own right as excellent comic writing.

Because it is grounded in reality (see pages 21–23), like the other scripts collected together here, it should prove thought-provoking as well as entertaining and may raise a number of points for discussion, just a few of which are suggested in the follow-up activities at the end of the book.

Comedy and Realism

How realistic need a comedy series be? There are those who like a series to be quite fantastic and to include bizarre happenings which would be quite impossible in real life. Others feel that a key feature of true situation comedy is that it should have a degree of realism. The President of ABC Television in the United States, Frederick Pierce, has said, when speaking of his network's high audience figures: 'Our secret is that we have concentrated on comedies with characters who seem like real people.'

Precisely how real his comedies have been is perhaps a matter for debate. Among his 'hit' series have been *Happy Days, Charlie's Angels* and *Soap* (all seen in this country on ITV). Among his other series have been *Three's Company* (an American version of ITV's *Man About the House*) and *Kotter*, a school comedy starring John Travolta.

It is obviously a matter of personal preference for each viewer as to how much realism or authenticity he or she expects of a particular series. However, it is important that the viewer should be aware whether a particular series is true to life or not.

The reader of this book can make his or her own judgement on many of the scenes and characters in the shows included in this collection. An assessment of

Going Straight may be helped by this article which appeared in *Radio Times* in February 1978. It is by Frank Norman, author of the musical *Fings Ain't What They Used T'Be* and himself an ex-convict.

The years, months, weeks, days, hours and minutes have at last snailed by – the wily old lag has done his bird and is getting out. The screws and the governor will be as pleased to see the back of him as he will of them. But the chances of them never meeting again are the same as last time – slim.

On the morning of his release the old lag packs his kit and exchanges a solemn handshake with his cell mates.

'Cheerio, Bert – if yuh can't be good don't get captured.'

'Don't forget to go round an' ask my old woman why I ain't 'ad a letter lately.'

'Send us a Christmas card.'

They are delighted that he is getting out, but envious. Maybe they will meet again in another prison or even on the outside. But if they do, the chances are they will find that they have little in common. It is the running battle of wits with the screws that binds them together while they are inside.

Somehow he won't get around to keeping any of his promises. In no time at all he will have completely forgotten about the nick, his cell, his mates and the screws – if he remembered he'd probably go straight.

Release from the nick comes early in the morning, soon after the day shift of screws come on duty at 7.0 am. Having bolted his last plate of porridge (he is a firm believer in the old superstition that if you don't eat your last plate of skilly you'll be back for it) the old lag is escorted to the gate by the chief officer. His thin civvy suit feels as light as a feather compared to his prison uniform.

In his pocket are a few quid from public funds, a National Insurance card bereft of stamps and a railway warrant clearly stamped with the authority of HM Prison, just to make sure that the railway booking clerk knows he is dealing with an ex-con.

The old lag has learned how to survive in the nick so well

that for a moment the pleasant dreams about future bank robberies, Rolls-Royce Silver Clouds, and damson-taloned dames swathed in black satin are eclipsed by a sudden dread of being cast out into the cruel and turbulent outside world.

'Out you go and don't come back,' says the gate screw, and the luckless fellow steps to freedom feeling like a man who has resigned himself to being hanged, only to be stabbed by the hangman.

The pubs are not yet open, so first port of call is the nearest workmen's cafe for rashers and eggs, golden toast and hot sweet tea. If all that, after the plain prison diet, fails to make him throw up, he may emerge from the cafe feeling more inclined to have a last go at treading the straight and narrow path, in a world that he has even less time for than it has for him.

But the interview at the Labour Exchange (Job Centre) is none too encouraging. The dapper civil servant rips open the sealed envelope from the prison authorities. He looks up sharply from the letter, eyes the old lag disdainfully and snaps: 'What exactly are your qualifications?'

'Sewing mailbags, guv.'

'Is there no other work that you could do?'

The old recidivist musters a crafty smile and says: 'Can yuh fix me up wiv a job as barf orderly in 'Olloway, guv'nor?'

'This is no laughing matter,' the man reproves him. The old lag nods agreement. 'The unemployment problem is acute at the moment. All I can advise you to do is apply for Social Security – what's your address?'

'No fixed abode, guv.'

'You cannot apply for Social Security unless you have a permanent address.'

'I'm nearly flat skint, guv,' the old lag explains. 'How can I get meself a place to live wivaht no lolly for the rent?'

'You'll just have to get a bed in a workingmen's hostel.'

'Doss 'ouses are worse'n the nick.' The old lag gets up, grins at the civil servant, scratches his gut and walks out.

In the local boozer that night things finally begin to look up. He is greeted on all sides like a conquering hero just home from the Thirty Years War – on and off, he has probably been away that long since he left school.

'Watcha, Bert, wen did yuh get aht?'

'Ave a drink old mate – nice to see yuh.'

In no time at all the pints of beer and double scotches are double-banked on the bar, and the piano player is pounding out the old favourites. Old ladies show their bloomers as they kick their varicose legs in the air to 'Knees Up Mother Brown' and with any luck there'll be a really good punch-up to round off the evening.

Surrounded by his mates at the bar the old lag, now four sheets to the wind, boasts loudly of his exploits in the nick and all the big jobs he's got lined up for the near future.

'There's this luverly little jewellers over 'Atton Garden wot's just arstin' to get turned over. A geezer wot I shared a peter wiv put me in abaht it – give me the 'ole layaht of the burglar-alarm system.'

The off-duty detective sergeant enjoying a pint in the saloon bar cocks an attentive ear, and smiles broadly at a private joke. If the old lag doesn't get his collar felt by the end of the week for loitering with intent to commit a felony, he'll start feeling homesick – home to him being a place that, when he goes there, makes him sicker than ever.

The Writers

Carla Lane

Carla Lane is one of the very small number of women who have written successful comedy series. Besides creating *The Liver Birds* she has also written the series *Butterflies* for BBC Television.

In November 1978, she wrote in the *Radio Times* about herself and about the place of women in television:

I entered the bewildering world of television just as woman had begun to shake her fragile fist in the face of man. I disappeared into that creative mincer and was so busy trying to emerge still looking and feeling like a woman that I seemed to miss it all. When the handle was finally turned, and I fell to the ground clutching my first cheque, I discovered that a new breed of female had grown up around me. They were brave and abandoned: they fought with frightened ferocity for all the things which I had accidentally achieved – equal pay, equal rights and individuality. Moved by their endeavours, I cheered them on as they treated the world to their thin soprano voice. 'A woman's place is *not* in the home,' they shrieked. It was convenient for me to agree as I was working in London and my home was in Liverpool, my family had booked in at the local chip shop, my Irish wolfhound had dug a hole in the garden and was sulking in it, the family parrot had hacked its way out of the house and was now living on top of the television aerial. A grave tug-of-war had begun inside me, excuses like 'talent', 'fulfilment', 'loyalties', 'personal need' were counteracted with words like 'priorities', 'duty', and all those other words which march over the hill with drawn swords just as you are about to climb it.

I had developed that despised disease – guilt.

John Chapman

John Chapman trained as an actor at the Royal Academy of Dramatic Art, and after two or three years on the stage he decided to try to write for the theatre. After the success of his first play, *Dry Rot*, which ran for nearly four years in London, he concentrated on playwrighting. His next play, *Simple Spyman*, also ran for three years. Then followed *The Brides of March* and *Diplomatic Baggage*.

Since the early 1960s he has written over 180 television comedies, including the *Hugh and I* series starring Terry Scott and Hugh Lloyd, and *Happy Ever After* on which he collaborated with Eric Merriman. Ten years ago he collaborated with Ray Cooney to write the stage play *Not Now Darling*. Subsequently they wrote *My Giddy Aunt*, *Move Over Mrs Markham* and *There Goes the Bride*. His last West End play was written with Anthony Marriott and was called *Shut Your Eyes and Think of England*. He is at present working on a new television series for the BBC.

Eric Merriman

Eric Merriman was, he says, born at an early age and educated at a grammar school and the Windmill Theatre.

He created the radio comedy series, starring Kenneth Horne, called *Beyond Our Ken*. He wrote this series for seven years and also wrote radio material for Morecambe and Wise, Ronnie Corbett and Ian Carmichael.

Apart from writing *Happy Ever After*, for television he has written material for *Sunday Night at the Palladium*, Tommy Steel Specials, Petula Clark, Dick Emery, Bruce Forsyth, Beryl Reid and Perry Como. More recently he has written the *Sammy Davis and Bruce Forsyth Special* for London Weekend Television and the *Dick Emery Comedy Hour* for Thames Television.

He is married with one son and homes in Hampstead Garden Suburb and Suffolk.

Eric Chappell

Eric Chappell was born in Grantham and is still living there. His first play was *The Banana Box* which was presented at Hampstead Theatre Club for a Sunday night performance in November 1970 and has subsequently been staged at the Phoenix Theatre, Leicester; the Theatre Royal, Newcastle; and Oxford Playhouse, prior to a successful West End run. *Rising Damp* was based on this play.

Since then he has had a number of his plays televised, including *The Spanish Dancers* and *We're Strangers Here* (now also a stage play). He also wrote the television serial *The Squirrels*, and the comedy series *Only When I Laugh*. A number of his plays have also been presented on radio.

Some years ago he gave up his job as an auditor with the Electricity Board to become a full-time writer.

Roy Clarke

Roy Clarke is in his late 40s and lives in splendid isolation in a converted mill in Sykehouse, a remote village in Yorkshire. He has a grown-up son and daughter, three dogs and two cats.

Before turning to full-time writing (in 1968), he had had a very varied career including teaching in a secondary modern school, two years with a county police force and odd jobs as a door-to-door salesman, office clerk and part-time taxi driver.

His first work was for radio: two thriller serials (both produced by Alan Ayckbourn) and a single play called *The World Of Miss Edwina Finch's Cat*. His first work for television was an episode of *The Trouble-Shooters* for BBC Television. He has written several other single plays and series including *Falling Star* (1970), *The Regulars* (1973), *The Bass Player and the Blonde* (1977), and *Flickers* (1980).

It was in 1972 that he first turned his attention to situation comedy, and the pilot episode of *Last of the Summer Wine* was transmitted in 1973. He also wrote a great deal of material for Ronnie Barker between 1972 and 1975 including the BBC Television series *Open All Hours* and since then he has written the series *Rosie* and *Potter*.

Dick Clement and Ian la Frenais

Dick Clement and Ian la Frenais form one of our most successful and creative comedy 'teams'. Together they have written *The Likely Lads* and *Whatever Happened to the Likely Lads?*, two Geordie situation comedy series; and also for BBC Television, *Porridge* and *Going Straight*. Besides these series, they have written for the *Ronnie Barker Playhouse* and *Comedy Playhouse* on BBC Television, and the series *Thick as Thieves* for London Weekend Television.

Their series *On the Rocks* was written for American television, for which they have also written numerous other shows.

Together they have written a number of film scripts including *The Jokers, Otley, Hannibal Brooks, Villain, Prisoner of Zenda* and *To Russia with Elton*, as well as the cinema versions of *The Likely Lads* and *Porridge*.

Dick Clements is also a film and television director and Ian la Frenais a producer.

Notes on Presentation

Even an informal classroom reading of a script is helped by rehearsal. Remember, not even the experienced professional actor is happy to sight-read, but usually prefers to have the chance to look over his part before a first reading in front of his colleagues. So, once a script has been cast, those who will be reading should be given the chance to look over their lines, make sure that they know when to pause; when to 'come in quickly' at the end of the previous speech; and to check that they appreciate the moods of their characters.

It is much easier to read to a class from the front of a traditional classroom, and from a standing position or a position where you can be seen by your audience. It may be useful to appoint a director who will decide the location of various settings and rehearse the actors in basic movements, checking that they know when and where to enter and exit.

Note that it is possible for a class to break up into groups, and for each group to rehearse its own interpretation of a script, and then for the groups to present their readings in turn to the whole class.

Even if you have seen the television production of any of the shows, resist the temptation to copy the screen version. Study the scripts and devise your own new productions.

In preparing the scripts for inclusion in this book, I have modified some of the film and studio directions so that when the scripts are being read aloud these directions (along with scene titles and descriptions of settings) can be read aloud by an announcer. In a class-room presentation, it might be helpful if he or she were in view of the audience but away from the acting area.

Note that, provided these directions are read sympathetically, a television script will read as fluently in the classroom as will a radio or stage play; but it should not be forgotten that (like any good television play) it was conceived in visual terms. It will therefore be fruitful to discuss (as the original director must have done) where and how each scene should be 'shot' to realize the author's intentions.

It will also be instructive to work out which scenes were recorded in a studio, and for which scenes it was necessary to go filming on location.

Another way of presenting these scripts is to record them on audio tape. The following points may be of help when recording:

(*a*)   Discover the directional qualities of your micro-phone – that is, from how wide an angle it picks up sound.

(*b*)   Even the best microphone cannot produce a good recording over a long distance from the sound source. For speech, it should be 30–40 cm from the mouth. (Those readers with stronger voices can obviously be further away than those who do not project well.)

(*c*)   It is much easier to record a play with actors standing rather than sitting. (They can then easily tip-toe away when not involved in a dialogue, and so allow those who are speaking to stand in the best positions.)

(*d*)   Do not hold the script between mouth and micro-phone, and avoid rustling pages.

(*e*)   Rooms with bare walls are unsuitable for making

recordings in, as they produce a lot of echo. Where possible, use a carpeted, curtained room (unless of course an echo effect is required!).

(*f*) It is possible to minimize echo (and also to lessen back-ground noise) by speaking closer to the microphone and by turning down the recording level. When doing this, a better sound may be achieved by speaking across the microphone rather than directly into it.

(*g*) Sound effects are important in any taped play. Don't worry about including every sound, but concentrate on those background noises which suggest location (for example, traffic noises, bus interiors, etc.) and sounds which indicate the arrival or departure of a character. Avoid clumsy and accidentally comic sounds (like artificial footsteps) to clutter or confuse the much more important dialogue.

(*h*) Gently fading out the very last few words or sounds of a scene and fading in the first sounds of a new scene will suggest a transition from one scene to another.

Acknowledgements

For permission to publish the plays in this volume, the editor and publishers are grateful to the following authors and their agents: Carla Lane and Jonathan Clowes Ltd for *The Liver Birds*; John Chapman and Eric Merriman, John Chapman Plays Ltd and Richard Stone for *Happy Ever After*; Roy Clarke and Sheila Lemon Ltd for *Last of the Summer Wine;* Dick Clement, Ian la Frenais and Witzend Productions for *Going Straight*.

No performance of these plays may be given unless a licence has been obtained. Applications should be addressed to the authors' agents.

Photographs on pages 34, 64, 124 and 148 are BBC copyright; the photograph on page 94 © Trident Television 1977.

The Liver Birds
The Never-ending End

Carla Lane

First shown on BBC 1 on 5 March 1976

Characters

Sandra
Carol
Mrs Hutchinson, Sandra's mother
Mrs Boswell, Carol's mother
Mr Boswell
Grandad Boswell
Lucian, Carol's brother
A policeman
Father O'Leary, a Catholic priest
Nellie Parker

Sandra (Nerys Hughes) and Carol (Elizabeth Estensen) in The Liver Birds (BBC copyright)

The Never-ending End

---

1 The living room of the girls' flat

Sandra *is ironing.* **Carol** *is sitting on the settee, writing a letter.*

There is a record playing of Brian Ferry – 'Sea Breezes'. **Sandra** *is listening in a dreamy fashion.* **Carol** *is surrounded by screwed up pieces of paper, and as we listen to the music she tears off another sheet, screws it up and throws it on to the floor. She starts another letter.*

We are now at the point in the song where the singer reaches the lines 'In love, in love', repeating it with a long plaintive echo, 'In love'.

Carol: [*Shrieking, out of tune*] In l-o-v-e.

Sandra: Carol – do you mind?

Carol: Sorry.

[*Pause and more music*]

Sandra: It's so beautiful, the song – so meaningful.

Carol: [*Writing*] Yeah.

Sandra: It's real – and sad – and true.

Carol: Oh, yeah.

Sandra: There would be no quality to life if we didn't

have other people to compose and sing our thoughts and feelings for us.

Carol: No.

Sandra: I mean, just listen to the pathos in that music.

Carol: [*Gets up and switches the record off*] I'm sorry Sandra, it's either his pathos or mine – I can't cope with both. [*She goes back to the settee*] Play it later when I've finished my letter – then I'll lie down on the settee, cut my main artery, and ebb away with him. [*She writes.* **Sandra** *irons*]

Sandra: I hope you realize the cost of writing paper.

Carol: Yeah, I've just done-in a week's wages.

Sandra: What exactly is bothering you?

Carol: [*Picks up one of the crumpled pieces of paper*] I'm trying to be casual, that's all. Does this sound OK? [*She reads*] 'Dear Ray, It was smashing to bump into you yesterday – after all this time – and didn't we have a laugh at the Safari Park. Ring me if you feel like it, and p'raps we'll do it again – I'm sorry that monkey pinched your wing mirrors. See you. Love, Carol.

Sandra: Oh, very romantic. I mean, couldn't you put some poetry into it?

Carol: Well, there's nothing very poetic about sitting in a car with a dozen monkeys slowly dismantling it, is there? [*Pause*] What would you put, then?

Sandra: I'd put: 'My dear Ray, It was so exciting meeting you yesterday – I shall always remember the lovely time you gave me – and those special moments in your car, outside my flat, how quickly the time passed. . . .'

Carol: Hang on – hang on – what special moments, in his car, outside my flat?

Sandra: I happened to notice, that's all. I happened to notice this red Volkswagen, the radio was on, and the windows were all steamed up. I thought Frank Sinatra was going to choke to death on his last song.

Carol: Nosey cow. Didn't you and Paul have anything better to do, then?

Sandra: Paul and I, Carol, have outgrown all that nonsense – grassy banks and backs of cars. We've moved on. Paul and I feel a deep peace when we're together. We don't have to *say* anything, we just *know*.

Carol: Know what?

Sandra: Well, we know that if there's one thing we'll never know, it's the answer to why we're able to sit in a room feeling peaceful, and knowing what we know.

Carol: Oh, I see. If only you'd said that in the first place, I could have gone insane a minute earlier.

Sandra: It's too difficult to explain, Carol.

Carol: It's OK. I think I've got it – you and Paul are too sophisticated to snog in the back of a car.

Sandra: Right.

Carol: You need civilized surroundings like a centrally heated flat, and the mind-blowing knowledge that somewhere, in a darkest corner – there lies a bed.

Sandra: Well, yeah, but. . . .

Carol: But you cast all sinful thoughts aside and watch other people snogging in the back of cars instead.

[*The phone rings*]

Sandra: [*Going to the phone*] That is not the case at all. [*She picks up the receiver*] Hello. [*There is a silence:* **Sandra** *registers an expression of horror and replaces the phone quickly*] It's heavy breathing.

Carol: Why didn't you put him on to me?

Sandra: Well, he didn't say who he wanted to breathe to, did he?

Carol: There are ways of dealing with those people, Sandra: either you keep them hanging on until they faint, or you give them a piece of your mind to let them see you're not afraid.

Sandra: But I *am* afraid – I mean it's somebody with a funny mind, isn't it, and they've singled us out. It's a disturbing thought.

Carol: Don't be daft, they don't single you out – they just mow their way through the directory. It just happens to be our turn today.

Sandra: [*Going back to the ironing board*] I don't know how you can be so flippant about it, Carol – he could be a complete lunatic – he could be across that road in the phone box, watching us with a pair of binoculars that zoom in and take all our clothes off. [*Pause*] In colour.

Carol: Oh shurrup, Sandra, let me get on with my letter.

Sandra: All right, all right, but remember – it might be *you* he's after.

Carol: It won't be me – it's your chest again. He's seen it running for a bus.

Sandra: Why is my chest blamed for everything?

Carol: Because it's usually the cause of everything. Look what happened to the milkman yesterday – he was mesmerized by it.

Sandra: Your imagination is running riot again.

Carol: So was his milk float.

[*The phone rings again*]

Sandra: ıt's him ... it's him. [**Carol** *gets up, takes the phone off the hook and puts it down. She goes back to her letter-writing*] What good will that do?

Carol: It'll run his phone bill up.

Sandra: [*Looks at the phone. She continues to iron but keeps glancing at the phone*] Oh, it's no good – I can't concentrate with him breathing all over the place. [*She goes to the phone and picks it up*] Excuse me, I don't know who you are, but you're a pathetic, despicable, evil-minded man. People like you should be locked away – people like you are a public menace – you're degrading – you're an animal – you're not fit to live in society – people like you.... [*She stops, listens and then cups her hand over the phone*] Carol, it's your Grandad.

Carol: [*Gets up and goes to phone*] Hello, Grandad – sorry about that – what is it, love?

Grandad: [*On the phone*] Is that you, our Carol?

Carol: Yeah, it's me.

Grandad: [*On phone*] They don't want me here.

Carol: What do you mean, 'They don't want me here'?

2 The Boswells' living room

Lucian *is sitting by the table: he has a piece of newspaper spread on it and on the newspaper, a rabbit.*

Grandad *is making his phone call. We can just see his rear end sticking out of the sideboard, where he has put the phone in the hope he will not be overheard.*
Lucian *is absorbed with grooming his rabbit.*

Mrs Boswell: [*Sticking her head round the door*] What's he doing?

Lucian: Making a phone call.

Mrs Boswell: [*Taps* **Grandad**] Don't be too long – your chair'll go cold. [*She goes out*]

Grandad: [*In cupboard*] It's because I'm old – they don't care – they don't love me – listen – I've got to go – it's freezing in the sideboard. [*We hear him put the phone down. He scrambles to his feet and is quite breathless with the effort*]

Mrs Boswell: [*Enters with a hot water bottle*] I've filled the hot water bottle to put down your vest.

Grandad: [*Hobbles to his chair*] Thanks. [*He flops down*]

Mrs Boswell: [*Handing the bottle to him*] Here.

Grandad: Thanks. [*Pause*] I'm not long. . . .

Mrs Boswell: '. . . for this world'. We know. You keep saying.

Mr Boswell: [*Enters from the hall. He is carrying a six-foot-tall plant in a pot*] Who keeps putting me weeping pear plant in the hall?

Mrs Boswell: I do. There isn't enough room for the people in this house – never mind that thing.

Grandad: It's me that's in the way – I know – I know.

Mr Boswell: [*Indicating* **Lucian**'s *rabbit*] There's room for his rabbits though, isn't there? Oh yes, there's room for them. [*To* **Lucian**] You put rabbits in hutches – fields – holes – not on tables. You put *food* on tables – food and drink. [*He plonks his plant in the middle of the table*] And plants. [*He goes to* **Mrs Boswell**] The only time you put rabbits on tables is when they're in pies. [*He goes to his chair opposite* **Grandad**'s *and sits in it*]

Mrs Boswell: [*To* **Mr Boswell**] I suppose you're there for the day now, are you? [*Indicates* **Grandad**] Look at them – father and son – sitting there like a couple of egg-bound battery hens.

Grandad: I'll go somewhere one day, somewhere quiet like elephants do, and I'll slip away, unnoticed.

Mrs Boswell: You'll have to get the hand-brake fixed on your armchair first. [*The canary tweets*] Tweet, tweet, my luverly.

3   The girls' flat

Sandra *is folding her ironing away.* **Carol** *is just finishing her letter: she is surrounded by even more screwed up pieces of paper.*

Carol: Right, that's it. [*She reads*] 'Dear Ray, thank you for a lovely day. Love, Carol.'

Sandra: Oh, very good. He can't fail to notice your literary powers.

Carol: I hope I see him again. We had a smashing time.

Sandra: Hey, you're really keen, aren't you? Love-struck again?

Carol: He told me I had an unusual face.

Sandra: So you have.

Carol: And he said my eyes were like brown velvet.

[**Sandra** *is busy folding the ironing*] Hey!

Sandra: Sorry, what?

Carol: He said my eyes were like brown velvet.

Sandra: Oh, very profound.

Carol: And he likes my 'wuffy' teeth.

Sandra: I've always told you, prominent teeth can be very attractive.

Carol: Yeah, as long as only one of you has them – otherwise when you kiss each other it sounds like colliding crockery.

Sandra: Come on, let's pick all these up. [*She begins to collect the screwed up letters*]

Carol: [*Thoughtfully*] I suppose me Grandad kissed somebody once.

Sandra: Well, of course he did, otherwise how did your father get here?

Carol: I suppose he wrote love-letters – to me Granny – and stole naughty moments in the chip shop doorway.

Sandra: Yes – there's a best-seller in all of us.

Carol: It must be awful when it all ends.

Sandra: No, Mother Nature compensates for all that: she sends out less adrenalin, she produces less hormones, you have less energy, less desire. Instead of looking forward to what you're going to do, you look back on what you've done.

Carol: [*Screws letter up*] I'm going to write another letter.

Sandra: Another one!

Carol: Yeah, a real passionate one.

Sandra: But Carol, you might put him off.

Carol: I might just turn him on – and if I'm going to end up like me Grandad, with nothing to think about but what I've done, I'd better do something worth thinking about, hadn't I?

4   The girls' flat

It is late the same evening. **Mrs Hutchinson** *and* **Mrs Boswell** *are sitting on the settee.* **Mrs Boswell** *is weeping into a handkerchief.*

Mrs Boswell: I'd only just filled his hot water bottle and the next thing, he's vanished. No word, nothing, vanished. [*She sniffles into her handkerchief*] I'm sorry, I always seem to be crying when you're here.

Mrs Hutchinson: We all shed tears, Mrs Boswell – it's the common denominator. Some of us do it privately – [**Mrs Boswell** *lets out a special wail*] some of us use the loud-hailer system.

Sandra: [*Entering*] There now, Mrs Boswell, drink some coffee.

Mrs Boswell: The room looks wrong without him – you can see the fire.

Sandra: P'raps he's just gone for an evening stroll.

Mrs Boswell: The last stroll he took was three months ago. He went to put the milk bottles out and we had to carry him back.

Sandra: He can't have gone very far then, can he? I'm sure Mr Boswell will ring any minute to say he's found him.

   [**Mrs Boswell** *gets her bottle of gin and a cup out of*

her handbag and pours herself a drink. **Mrs Hutchinson** *looks disdainfully at her*]

Mrs Hutchinson: Sandra, darling, get Mrs Boswell a glass, will you? [**Mrs Boswell** *pours out more gin*] Or a vase.

Mrs Boswell: No thanks, I'm more at home with cups.

Sandra: I'm sorry Carol isn't here, only she got this phone call from Ray, you see – he's her new boyfriend.

Mrs Boswell: And our Barbara away for the weekend – me hour of need and not a daughter in sight. [*Pause*] Did she say when she'd be back, our Carol?

Sandra: No, she didn't actually. She stood in the doorway and she said, 'Yippy, yippy, yum yum yum – look out, world, here I come!'

Mrs Hutchinson: [*Drily*] Oh well, we can expect her back any minute then, can't we?

Mrs Boswell: I don't know what I've done to deserve all this worry. I just can't keep the family together at all. I've spent my whole married life charging about like a bloody sheepdog.

Mrs Hutchinson: Yes, well, I think you're too soft with them. After all, you're an individual – you have a mind and you ought to use it. To hell with it all, I say – hurl a vat of scouse on the stove and dash out and buy yourself a new headscarf. [*She laughs.* **Mrs Boswell** *remains very grave*] Oooh – I'm flogging a dead sheepdog here.

Mrs Boswell: 'I'll go somewhere one day,' he said, 'somewhere quiet like the elephants do – and I'll slip away, unnoticed.'

Mrs Hutchinson: Yes, well, they're only words, aren't they?

Sandra: Daddy's always threatening to leave home, isn't he, Mummy?

Mrs Hutchinson: Yes – but he never does. I always beat him to it.

Mrs Boswell: It's hard being a woman, it's cruel being a woman. Women are beasts of burden.

Mrs Hutchinson: When men marry us, they throw a saddle on our backs and point up towards the hurdles of life.

Mrs Boswell: [*Tipping the gin bottle over cup*] I've run out of gin.

Sandra: P'raps it's just as well – you've got another hurdle coming up, and we don't want you nobbled, do we?

5 The girls' flat

It is the following morning. It is still dark. The front door opens: **Carol** *lets herself in very carefully. She closes the door and tip-toes towards the living room. The light goes on.*

Sandra: [*Standing in the bedroom doorway, angrily*] And where do you think you've been?

Carol: Oh, God, Sandra — me stomach's gone into me boots.

Sandra: [*Going to her*] It's seven o'clock in the morning. I've been up all night — where've you been?

Carol: Oh — around.

Sandra: Around! Around what — the world?

Carol: [*Starts to take her coat off*] I would've phoned you, but Ray doesn't have a phone. [*Walks into the bedroom.* **Sandra** *follows her*]

Sandra: You mean you've been in his flat — all night?

Carol: [*Lies down on her bed*] Yeah, isn't it shocking — I did explain about the non-meat-eating, non-smoking, non-drinking, whiter than white friend of mine.

Sandra: Have you no thought for others?

Carol: Look, who do you think you are, me mam or something? I thought we both left home to escape this sort of thing.

Sandra: Your Grandad went out last night.

Carol: Good – I'm glad somebody had a good time. And if it's any consolation to you, I didn't do anything I can spend my old age gloating about. We had a candle-lit supper, opened a very noisy bottle of champagne – and the next thing I knew his dog was having pups all over the flat. [*She gets under the bed clothes, then peeps out again*] Dog and pups all doing well – dog owner not doing very well – dog owner's girl friend spent the night nursing all nine of them! [*She gets back under the bed clothes*]

[*Pause*]

Sandra: He didn't come back, your grandfather.

Carol: [*Sitting up*] Didn't come back? But that's silly, me Grandad never leaves his armchair. Have they looked under the cushions?

Sandra: It's serious, Carol. The police are looking for him.

Carol: Didn't he say where he was going?

Sandra: No, he just went.

Carol: It's my fault – I should have taken notice of that phone call yesterday.

Sandra: You mustn't blame yourself, he was always imagining he wasn't wanted – old people do that sort of thing. [*Pause*] What are you doing now?

Carol: [*Getting up*] I'm going to the police station.

Sandra: Your father has done all that.

Carol: Me Dad doesn't get on with the police. He'll annoy them so much that if they do find me Grandad, they'll take him out and lose him again. [*She goes into the living room*]

Sandra: [*Following* **Carol** *to the living room*] But, Carol, you haven't had any sleep.

Carol: Yes, I have – there was a lull between the third and fourth pups.

6   The police station

A **Policeman** *stands behind the desk: he is writing in a large book.* **Mr Boswell** *is sitting on a bench opposite: he is smoking a cigarette. There are cigarette ends all over the floor around his feet. Next to him sits* **Mrs Boswell**. *Next to her is* **Lucian**. **Lucian** *has his long fur coat on and a fur hat.*

Mr Boswell: [*Pointing aggressively towards the* **Policeman**] Catch the criminals, that's what I say. Catch the criminals. [*The* **Policeman** *cringes, but continues to write. Pause*] Never mind the paper work, get your pandas out and run the criminals down. [*Silence. The* **Policeman** *closes the book*] Finished yer memoirs, have yer? Going for yer cup of tea now, are yer? [*The phone rings*] Oh dear, there's the phone. Another master criminal motorist has been found with a faulty ash-tray.

[*With huge restraint, the* **Policeman** *picks up the phone*]

Mrs Boswell: I don't know how you can sit there annoying that poor man. And you with no brakes on yer bike.

Mr Boswell: If I'd been in charge, I'd have found him by now.

Mrs Boswell: You can't even find yer own back pocket.

[*The door opens:* **Carol** *and* **Sandra** *rush in.* **Carol** *goes straight to the* **Policeman**, *takes the phone from him and hands it to* **Sandra**]

Carol: Excuse me – I've lost me Grandad.

[*The* **Policeman** *gazes helplessly at her*]

Mrs Boswell: It's our Carol.

[**Carol** *goes to the family.* **Sandra** *looks at the* **Policeman**]

Carol: Is there any news?

Sandra: [*Smiles at the* **Policeman** *then speaks into the phone*] I'm so sorry but my friend has lost her Grandad, you see. I'll put you back on to him now. [*She hands the phone to the* **Policeman**. *He goes to speak into it, but* **Sandra** *interrupts*] I apologize for my friend, she's a bit upset, she and her boyfriend didn't manage to get to bed last night.

Policeman: [*Bewildered*] Oh. [*He is about to speak into the phone again when* **Carol** *charges up and takes the phone from him. She replaces the receiver*]

Carol: [*Urgently*] When are you going to find him? When are you going to find me Grandad?

Policeman: It may have escaped your notice, but I was on the telephone, darlin'.

Carol: There's no time to be on the phone – why aren't you out looking for him!

Policeman: [*With huge sarcasm*] We are looking for him, it's just that somebody has to be here to answer the phone – in case somebody else needs us, you know, the odd murder, things like that.

[**Carol** *looks at him: she is almost going to cry*]

Sandra: Don't cry, Carol. [*To* **Policeman** *as she steers* **Carol** *towards the bench*] Could she have a cup of tea and two rounds of toast, please?

[*The* **Policeman** *gazes in amazement.* **Sandra** *and* **Carol** *sit on the bench with the others: they all stare at the* **Policeman**. *He stares back. We see him gathering restraint. He comes from behind the counter, stands in front of them*]

Policeman: Now why don't you lovely people all go home and leave the rest to us? We've got all the details.

Mr Boswell: [*Stands up*] Details! He's not a purse, yer know – or an umbrella . . . he's a person . . . a human person.

Lucian: I think they'll have that written down, Dad.

Mr Boswell: [*To* **Lucian**, *mimicking him*] 'I think they'll have that written down, Dad' – do you have to talk like that?

Mrs Boswell: He talks the way you do – common.

Mr Boswell: [*To the* **Policeman**] Did you hear that? [*To* **Mrs Boswell**] He's not common – he's diabolical common. It's like living with a baritone duck.

[**Carol** *is still dabbing her eyes*]

Lucian: I'd like to sit and think about me Grandad, if you don't mind.

Mrs Boswell: It's a bit late now, isn't it? All this crying and thinking – you should have thought about him before.

Policeman: Now then, now then.

Mrs Boswell: [*Gets up, attacking the* **Policeman** *verbally*] I cooked for him, I made his bed for him, I cut his toenails for him – he was well looked after.

Policeman: [*Wilting under her attack*] I'm sure you did a very good job. . . .

Mr Boswell: [*To the* **Policeman**] How do you know?

Sandra: [*Gets up and joins them*] Now look, you're all getting a bit tense – after all, we have been up all night.

[*They are hemming the* **Policeman** *in now, against the front of his desk*]

Mr Boswell: [*Pointing to* **Mrs Boswell** *and addressing the* **Policeman**] She nagged him. [*To* **Mrs Boswell**] You nagged him. [*To the* **Policeman**] He was the nail – and she was the hammer.

Carol: [*Leaping up and joining the affray*] That's not true.

Mr Boswell: [*To the* **Policeman** *who is pressed against the counter, and just looks from one to another*] Bang, bang, bang, she went – every morning. I expected to get up and find his head sticking out of the floorboards.

Policeman: Now look, if you ask me. . . .

Mr Boswell: We're not asking you.

Carol: [*To* **Policeman**] My mam did everything for my Grandad.

Mr Boswell: [*To* **Carol**] You left home, didn't you – and last night you were out enjoying yourself.

Sandra: She was not enjoying herself, she was delivering puppies.

Mr Boswell: Funny time for people to have their dogs delivered, isn't it?

Policeman: Shut up!

Lucian: [*Gets up quietly. He goes to the* **Policeman** *who looks almost fearful as he approaches*] Do yer ever get any stray rabbits in?

[*The* **Policeman** *looks at* **Lucian**'s *fur hat and coat. He thinks he is imagining it all. A row starts, with all the members of the family shouting at each other.* **Mrs Hutchinson** *enters. She sweeps towards the* **Policeman**. *She is wearing her usual enormous feathered type hat. The* **Policeman**'s *face registers doom*]

Mrs Hutchinson: Good morning, dear man, have you heard any news yet about the mislaid person? [*To the others*] Oh, there you all are. [*The row stops. She looks at the rest. They are all grouped together,* *looking at her*] Isn't it marvellous how a tragedy unites a family.

[*The row starts again*]

7 The girls' flat

It is a little later in the day. **Carol** *is curled up on the settee fast asleep.*
The kettle whistles in the kitchen. **Carol** *leaps up from the settee, rushes to the phone and picks it up.*

Carol: Hello, I'm here. Have you found him?

Sandra: [*Entering*] It's the kettle. [*She goes to the kitchen. The kettle stops whistling*]

Carol: Oh.

Sandra: [*Entering with a dish*] I've made you something to eat – come on. It's leek and green peppers in cheese sauce.

Carol: Isn't there any meat?

Sandra: You know I can't cook animals, Carol.

Carol: [*Gazes into dish*] It's like giving a dog a salad.

Sandra: Wouldn't it be nice if you simply said 'Thank you, Sandra. That's very kind of you, Sandra. I do appreciate it, Sandra.'

Carol: Thank you, Sandra. That's very kind of you, Sandra. I do appreciate it, Sandra. [*She tastes the food*] Ugh! [*She pushes the plate away*]

Sandra: I know you're under stress, Carol, but it hasn't been much fun for me either. I think I've been very tolerant. After all, it's not my Grandad that's missing.

Carol: Sorry.

Sandra: And *I* didn't get any sleep last night either.

Carol: No, sorry.

Sandra: And I have given up seeing Paul today.

Carol: Yes, yes, sorry.

Sandra: I mean, you know me. I'm not one to complain, but if you're going to sit there hurling abuse at my leek pie. . . .

Carol: [*Shouting*] All right, all right! [*She gets up and goes into the bedroom.* **Sandra** *picks up the dish and a spoon and follows* **Carol**. **Carol** *sits on her bed*]

Sandra: A whole hour it took me. [*No response*] You know how I hate cooking. The only thing that spurred me on was the anticipated pleasure of seeing that dish empty.

Carol: [*Takes the dish, empties it on to the floor, and hands* **Sandra** *the dish back*] One empty dish.

Sandra: [*Fuming. Gazes at the mess on the carpet*] You - you - [*Pause while she struggles for words*] Well, I'll tell you something, Carol Boswell - I'm getting just a little bit tired of your family. First your father disappears, then Barbara, now your Grandad - it's a wonder your poor mother doesn't turn them all loose with pierced ears and tambourines.

Carol: Your family hasn't been exactly trouble-free, has it?

Sandra: At least Mummy and Daddy only have *one* problem - your lot could keep Marjorie Proops employed for life.

Carol: My family's problems keep your mother occupied, don't they? Whenever the show starts, she's always there, isn't she - sitting in the front row, blocking the view with her bloody hat!

[*The girls stare at each other: both back down. There is a silence as* **Sandra** *takes the dish and spoon and begins to scrape up the food off the carpet*]

Carol: [*Quietly*] I'll have it later.

Sandra: As you wish.

[*Pause*]

Carol: I love him, you know – me Grandad.

Sandra: Yes.

Carol: When you love people – you're stuck with them, aren't you?

Sandra: I suppose so, yes.

Carol: He's probably missing me Granny – thirty-eight years they were married. [*She stops and thinks*] Sandra?

Sandra: What?

Carol: What date is it?

Sandra: The sixth.

Carol: So yesterday was the fifth.

Sandra: That's highly probable – yes.

Carol: I think I know where he went.

Sandra: Where?

Carol: Yesterday was their wedding anniversary.

Sandra: So?

Carol: He might have gone to see her.

8   A cemetery

Carol *and* **Sandra** *walk into the cemetery grounds and along one of the paths.*

Sandra: But even if he did come to see her, he wouldn't still be here, would he?

Carol: You don't know, do you? He thinks nobody wants him.

Sandra: I've just remembered, your mother said that your Grandad said, 'One day I'll go to a quiet place – like the elephants do.'

Carol: Elephants go somewhere to die, don't they?

Sandra: Yes.

Carol: I wouldn't put it past him – if he can find a way to cut down expenses, he will.

Sandra: When did he last come?

Carol: The day of the funeral – he married his armchair after that. But he often talked about coming.

Sandra: [*Looks round the cemetery*] Ooh, Carol. All these poor people, isn't it sad?

Carol: Yeah, we'll end up like this one day.

Sandra: When I die I'm not going to have a big stone with my age written all over it.

Carol: Don't worry, love, I'll see that you go in the proper manner – instead of a headstone we'll put a water trough; little dogs can come and drink from it, little birds can come and bathe in it, me goldfish can come and spend his holidays in it, and when you have visitors, they can sit and soak their feet in it. [*She stops suddenly as they come to a very tatty grave. It has a tree about four foot high, which is black-branched and obviously has been dead for some time. The headstone is dark, and the writing obscured*] This is me Granny's grave. [**Sandra** *looks moved.* **Carol** *drops to her knees and makes the sign of the cross*]

Sandra: [*A whisper*] Do you want me to do it too?

Carol:　No, members only.

Sandra:　[*Goes to the other side of the grave, and kneels opposite* **Carol**] Your Grandad hasn't been, has he?

Carol:　It doesn't look like it.

　[*Pause*]

Sandra:　It's very untidy, isn't it?

Carol:　Yeah, but me Granny likes things that way, her home was just the same – an old aspidistra in the window, tins of conny-onny on the table, washing under the stairs, potato peelings in the sink. [*She peers at the grave, addressing her granny*] I don't suppose you know where your old man is, do you, love?

Sandra:　Carol! You mustn't talk to her like that – not when she's dead.

Carol:　[*Gets up. She looks at her Granny's grave, then at the one next to it which is neat, and has masses of bunches of flowers on it. She looks along the row of graves: all the rest are tidy, the headstones bright*] It looks like the street she lived in – rows of neat little houses – all except hers. [*Looks at the tree*] Even the tree in her back yard looked like this one.

Sandra:　She's kept her personality. Not many people keep their personality once they're dead.

Carol:　Yeah. [*Looks at grave*] See yer, Gran.

Sandra:　[*Whispering*] 'Bye, nice to have met you.

Carol:　[*Passing, looking at the next grave and reading the words on the headstone*] 'Frederick Parker, departed this life April 4th 1959. Deeply mourned by his loving wife Nellie.' [*She picks up a* *vase of flowers from the Parker grave and places it on her Grandmother's grave*] There you are, love – a present from Nellie Parker. [*She walks away*]

Sandra: [*She is just about to get up when she notices a small tin lying amongst the weeds. She picks it up and studies it*] Hey, Carol! [**Carol** *stops and turns.* **Sandra** *gets up and runs to* **Carol**]

Carol: [*Taking the tin from* **Sandra**] Grandad's tobacco tin!

9   The Boswells' living room

Mrs Boswell *and* **Carol** *are kneeling in front of* **Father O'Leary**. **Mr Boswell** *is sitting in his armchair drinking whisky.* **Grandad**'s *tobacco tin is lying in the centre of the table.*

Father O'Leary: [*Praying*] . . . And we ask you, dear Father, to bestow thy loving care and protection upon these thy faithful servants. And we ask you for the safe return and blessed deliverance of. . . .

Sandra: [*Enters from the kitchen with tea on a tray*] Right! Tea up. [**Father O'Leary** *stops and waits with expression of resignation*] Sorry. [*She stands motionless with her tray*]

Father O'Leary: For the safe return and blessed deliverance of their dear one, so that their hearts may be joyful and their family may unite again in peace and love. Amen.

Mrs Boswell, Carol and Sandra: Amen.

Father O'Leary: Amen. . . . [*He waits for* **Mr Boswell** *who is busy drinking whisky. They all look at him*]

Mr Boswell: Amen.

Father O'Leary: [*Muttering*] There's one in every flock.

[**Sandra** *goes to place the tray on the table, but the presence of the tobacco tin makes it seem indelicate. Instead, she puts the tray on the sideboard, and sits by the table with* **Carol**]

Mrs Boswell: Thank you, Father, you're a great comfort to us all. Would you stay for some tea now?

Father O'Leary: No, thank you, Mrs Boswell. And the Lord said, 'On the seventh day thou shalt work twice as hard.' [*He goes towards the door*]

Carol: See you, Father.

Father O'Leary: Bless you, child. Is this a temporary visit to the fold, or an additional hazard to my job?

Carol: Temporary, Father.

Father O'Leary: [*To* **Sandra**] And will I ever have the pleasure of seeing you in the church?

Sandra: I don't go to church, Father, I'm a vegetarian.

Father O'Leary: Ah yes – well, we have stopped sacrificing cows now, you know. [*To* **Mrs Boswell**] I'll see myself out, Mrs Boswell. [*He looks at* **Mr Boswell** *who is silently drinking his whisky*] I'll pray for you – *and* your husband's stomach.

Carol, Sandra and Mrs Boswell: Thank you, Father. [*They all look at* **Mr Boswell**]

Mr Boswell: Thank you, Father.

[**Father O'Leary** *goes out.* **Mrs Boswell** *goes to the table and sits down. They stare at the tobacco tin*]

Sandra: [*Brightly*] Now you mustn't be sad – I'll pour the tea. [*She gets up and goes to tray. She has her back to them*]

Mrs Boswell: That was the only pleasure he had – his tobacco tin.

Carol: That – and his little book of rude jokes.

Sandra: You must bear up, be optimistic.

Mrs Boswell: He used to sit there, reading them out, during the news.

Carol: And then he'd laugh.

Mrs Boswell: And cough.

Carol: And he'd say, [*Imitating* **Grandad**] 'I'm not long for this world.'

[*Pause*]

Sandra: You must be brave.

Mrs Boswell: Just think – he must have been kneeling there, by the graveside, alone.

Carol: Rolling his last fag. [**Sandra** *suddenly breaks down.* **Carol** *goes to her*] Oh, love, sit down. [*She guides* **Sandra** *to the table*] Have a cup of tea.

Sandra: [*Tearfully*] Thank you.

Carol: You just sob into that, love. [*She gives* **Sandra** *a cup of tea*]

Mr Boswell: What did he go there for, anyway – to the cemetery?

Mrs Boswell: He went because it was his wedding anniversary. He felt lonely. He wanted somebody to talk to.

Mr Boswell: He never talked to her when she was alive.

Carol: Well he couldn't, could he? She wouldn't let him get a word in.

Mr Boswell: Where is he now, then, that's what I want to know. I can't afford to be drinking all this whisky.

Sandra: The trouble is you never know what a person might do when they're desperate. A friend of Mummy's was very depressed for a long time, and nobody took any notice of her – so she took all her clothes off and ran amok in the precinct.

Mrs Boswell: I hope he doesn't do that – it's not a pretty sight.

Mr Boswell: The human body might look very pleasant when it is stationary – but once it starts dashing about it looks bloody daft.

Lucian: [*Entering with a rabbit*] Dad, we saw a police car coming up the road.

Mrs Boswell: Oh, my God.

Lucian: If they bring a stray rabbit with them, I'll be out in the yard.

[*He goes out and* **Carol** *follows.* **Mrs Boswell** *opens her handbag, takes out her cup and takes out a bottle of gin. She pours a large drink.* **Mr Boswell** *pours himself another whisky*]

Mrs Boswell: [*Wailing*] Ooh, supposing he's dead.

Mr Boswell: I'll kill him if he isn't.

Carol: [*Re-entering*] Dad, they're stopping here.

Mrs Boswell: Ooh, Holy Mother – trouble finds its way to this house like flies to a dung heap.

Mr Boswell: [*To* **Mrs Boswell**] Will yer stop wailin'! How can I exercise me strength and courage with you carrying on like that? [*To* **Carol**] Yer mother will identify him.

Mrs Boswell: I can't, I can't. You do it, Carol. Tell them he was wearing a balaclava, two vests and a pair of our Lucian's Brer-Rabbit underpants.

Sandra: [*Bites her lips to stop crying*] Oh, Carol.

Carol: Pull yourself together, Sandra.

[**Carol** *goes out.* **Sandra** *takes Mrs Boswell's cup of gin, swallows it back, and hands* **Mrs Boswell** *the cup. She follows* **Carol**]

Mrs Boswell: I can't bear it. [*She puts the cup down and covers her face.* **Mr Boswell** *stands up, then sits down again*]

Mr Boswell: [*Stands up, then sits down again with a drunken expression*] I can't stand up.

10   The street outside the Boswells' house

A **Policeman** *is just helping* **Grandad** *towards the front door. It opens:* **Carol** *and* **Sandra** *are there.*

Carol: [*Angrily*] Grandad! Where've you been.

Sandra: [*Hugs* **Grandad**] Oh, Grandad!

Policeman: He *is* yours, then?

Carol: Yeah, he's ours. Thanks. [*The* **Policeman** *goes back to the car.* **Carol** *turns to* **Grandad**] Now we know where you went yesterday, Grandad – but where've you been all night?

Grandad: I went to the cemetery to have a word with her.

Sandra: But Grandad, you've got a house full of live

people who love you. The cemetery's full of . . . dead people.

[*The* **Policeman** *is now escorting an old lady towards them*]

Grandad: No, it's not.

Carol: Who's this?

Policeman: They said they were together.

Grandad: It's Nellie Parker.

Carol and Sandra: Nellie Parker!

Grandad: She was there having a word with *her* husband. [*Devilishly*] We went back to her place! [*He ushers* **Nellie Parker** *into the house. The girls are open-mouthed*]

Sandra: [*To* **Carol**] What was that you said, Carol – 'It must be awful when it all ends!'

[*They go into the house. The door shuts*]

The end

Happy Ever After

Foster Fletchers

John Chapman and
Eric Merriman

First shown on BBC1 on 9 September 1976

Characters

Terry Fletcher
June Fletcher, his wife
Aunt Lucy
Mr Truscott, a welfare officer
Anthony Simpson, a 12-year-old schoolboy
Truscott's secretary

Terry (Terry Scott) and June Fletcher (June Whitfield)
in the series Happy Ever After (BBC copyright)

Foster Fletchers

---

1 The Fletchers' sitting room

It is early evening. **June** *is standing on a pair of steps, hanging the last curtain hook on the rail, having just finished spring-cleaning the room.* **Lucy** *enters with a large cardboard box.*

Lucy: Oh, you've got the curtains back again all right?

June: Yes, I wanted to get this room straight before Terry's home. He can't bear spring-cleaning, and hates the thought of turning things out.

Lucy: I wish he felt the same about me. Did you want to keep this stuff we found in the attic?

June: Oh yes, dear. Don't throw that away.

Lucy: [*Putting the box down*] Everything gets so dusty, it's made my throat quite dry.

June: [*Climbing down*] Would you like another cup of tea, Lucy?

Lucy: No dear, don't bother. We'll just make do with a sherry.

June: Good idea. We've earned a drink.

Lucy: You sit down. I'll get it.

June: [*Kneels by the box and starts to open it*] I know it's probably silly to hang onto these toys the kids had, but you never know, they might come in handy for the grandchildren.

Lucy: [*Pouring the drinks*] It's a bit early to think of that. They're not married yet.

June: Who knows these days, they may not even do it in that order.

Lucy: [*She finishes pouring out the two glasses of sherry and looks at the bottle*] It's getting a bit low. Terry'll be needing some more soon. . . . Oh, that's funny.

June: What is it?

Lucy: [*Looking at the label*] There seems to be some sort of pencil mark on the bottle.

June: [*Puzzled*] What?

Lucy: Never mind. Two can play at that game. [*She picks up a pencil from the shelf and makes half a dozen other marks above and below the original one*] There, that'll give him something to think about. [*She puts the bottle back on the sideboard and brings the glasses over and gives one to **June**]

June: Thank you, dear, and bless you for all your help today. [**June** *takes a sip*]

Lucy: Well we can't have you working on your own, can we? [*She knocks her drink back in one, and then looks at her empty glass*] And we can't have you drinking on your own either. I'll join you. [*She returns to the sideboard and refills her glass*]

June: [*Pulling a furry animal out of the box*] Oh, look – old Fuzzy Wuzzy.

Lucy: [*Not turning round*] No, I'll be all right, dear.

June: That was Debbie's favourite, they were inseparable. How she loved him! [*Looks at it*] Least, I think it was a 'him'. [*She pulls out a doll*] Remember this, Lucy? You sent it to Susan on her first birthday, all the way from India.

Lucy: Goodness, did I really? You've got a good memory.

June: I couldn't forget. Terry christened her 'Nelly from Delhi'. [*They both chuckle.* **June** *then sighs*] Oh dear, happy days. [*She then rummages in the box again*]

Lucy: [*Picking up the doll*] Doesn't time fly? It seems like only yesterday when they were toddling around and sitting on my knee. They were such lovely children.

June: [*Takes out a rattle and holds it fondly*] Yes and now they've all grown up and left home. And it happened so quickly. They're young for such a short time.

[**June** *shakes the rattle gently.* **Lucy** *is also sitting down now, holding the doll and lost in reverie. The front door is heard to shut, followed by* **Terry** *singing casually*]

Terry: [*In the hallway*] 'I left my heart in San Francisco' [*Entering*] 'High on a hill I....' [*The song dies on his lips as he takes in the scene.* **Lucy** *is holding a doll and* **June** *is holding a rattle.* **Terry** *is open-mouthed. Speaks jovially*] Hello – have we fallen off the Magic Roundabout?

Lucy: What? Oh, hello, dear.

Terry: Evening. [*Then eyeing* **June** *who is still miles away*] June, it's me, I'm home.

June: Oh, Terry. [*She starts to cry*]

Terry: Oh, Gawd. Now what's the matter?

June: [*Sniffing*] Nothing. Look– [*She shakes the rattle gently in his face*]

Terry: [*Completely baffled*] How long have you been on the sherry? Hold on. [*He goes and picks up the sherry bottle*] Hello, who's been tampering with my Tio Pepe?

Lucy: [*Getting up and leaving the doll on the sofa*] I think I'll just go and lie down for a bit.

Terry: Well I should hurry up, it'll soon be dark, and you don't want to be out of your coffin when the moon rises.

[**Lucy** *goes out*]

June: Poor Lucy, she's tired out. We've been spring-cleaning all day.

Terry: Are you going to do this room tomorrow?

June: Oh Terry, can't you see a difference?

Terry: [*Looking round*] No.

June: You'd be surprised how much filth there was on these walls.

Terry: Lucy been at the graffiti again, has she?

June: I don't know why I bother. You never notice anything.

Terry: Well, I didn't have much chance. I walk in and what do I see? Old 'Days of Wine and Roses' sitting there with a baby's doll and you accompanying her on the maraccas.

June: It's Debbie's rattle. [*Points to the doll*] And that's Nelly from Delhi.

Terry: Who?

June: Don't you remember? And old Fuzzy Wuzzy and Mr Floppy-legs?

Terry: [*Worried*] June. love, when you were doing all this cleaning today you didn't get a bang on the head, by any chance?

June: There's nothing wrong with me. It's *your* memory that's gone. Look – [*She pulls an old teddy-bear out of the box*] Here's Mr Floppy-legs.

Terry: [*Remembering*] Oh, that Mr Floppy-legs. Why didn't you say so? Of course. Susan's wasn't it?

June: No, Frank's. It was always in bed with him.

Terry: I hope he's doing better than that now. Moth-eaten old thing, I don't wonder you're chucking all this rubbish out.

June: It's not rubbish and I wouldn't dream of throwing it away.

Terry: Well it's no good, is it? I mean, who'd want to go to bed with this? [*Holding up teddy-bear*]

June: That's not the point. All these things have a sentimental value. They belonged to our children, yours and mine. Don't you feel anything?

Terry: Yes, hungry. What's for supper?

June: I'll find something.

Terry: What d'you mean – find something? Just look in the oven, that's where it'll be.

June: I'm afraid it won't. I haven't had a moment today to think about things like that.

Terry: I must eat. Surely you've got something in the larder?

June: I think there's some veal and ham pie.

Terry: I had that for lunch.

June: Well, I'm not to know that, am I?

Terry: What d'you expect me to do then, phone in every day at lunch time? 'Hello, darling, I thought you'd just like to know I've had lentil soup for starters, now should I go for the steak pie or the fish, bearing in mind that for dessert I rather like the look of the –

June: [*Cutting in*] All right, no veal and ham pie. Tell you what we'll have – prawn cocktail, steak, jacket potatoes, salad, cheese and biscuits and coffee.

Terry: [*Cheerfully*] That's more like it.

June: Good. That's settled then.

Terry: Lovely. Have I got time for another drink? [*Goes to find his glass*]

June: Yes, but hadn't you better book the table first?

Terry: Right I'll – [*Stops*] What?

June: [*Looks at her watch*] About eight-thirty?

Terry: Oh, June, it's too expensive to keep going out for meals.

June: It didn't cost much the last time you took me out. It was only one pound, fifteen shillings and threepence – the silver threepence.

Terry: Look at it this way. Isn't it a compliment to you, as the chef, that I prefer to eat at this establishment? It's quiet, it's spotlessly clean – especially today. The cuisine is superb, and I fancy the waitress.

June: Well, thank you Egon Ronay, but the management regrets that tonight everything is off except the veal and ham pie.

Terry: Oh, all right then, we'll go out.

June: Thank you darling. [*She gives him a little kiss*]

Terry: Just one thing.

June: What?

Terry: If the bill is too exorbitant I shouldn't pay if I were you. [*He laughs*]

June: Anyway, when you think about it, there are only the two of us now. In the good old days you used to have to fork out for five.

Terry: Yes, thank goodness they're off our hands now.

June: Oh, don't say that. The kids used to love going out for a treat. Don't you remember how sweet they looked, all dressed up and sitting there, good as gold?

Terry: Yes, a fine bunch. A credit to me, they were.

June: Yes dear.

Terry: Mind you, I had to be firm at times. What a devil Frank could be!

June: Yes. Remember when he cut the tops off all your tulips?

Terry: And what happened? Straight up to his room, into bed, no supper, and there he stayed.

June: Until an hour later and then, remember, there was a little knock and a tiny tear-stained face peeped round the door. 'Can I come out now, Daddy? I'm sorry for what I did. And I promise tomorrow I'll glue them all back on again.'

Terry: [*Chuckling*] Yes, he did too. Wrong way up, mind you.

June: [*Fondly*] Ah, you couldn't ever really be cross with him. He just used to stand there with those big innocent eyes. [*She starts to get tearful*] I couldn't bear to see him unhappy and I just hated it when he cried.

Terry: I'm not mad about it when you do it either. That's the second time in five minutes. What's the matter with you?

June: Nothing.

Terry: You keep saying that. There must be something.

June: [*Sniffing*] No – it's just – just – happy memories. [*She cries again*]

Terry: Going to be a lovely dinner. If you keep that up you'll never finish your soup.

June: I'm sorry, darling. I *am* looking forward to going out. And I promise I won't cry any more. It was only because I came across this old box of toys and it reminded me of all the happy times we had as a family.

Terry: We still are a family.

June: It's not the same thing. Frank's miles away in Hong Kong. Debbie's right up north. . . .

Terry: But you've got Susan in Chelsea. That's only down the road.

June: Yes, but that's not the same as being with us – together – all of us, as a real family.

Terry: You've still got some of your family upstairs, remember? Baby Jane – and that mangy old mynah bird of hers, that's enough to be going on with. By the way, when is she going?

June: I don't know. She's been talking about it for the past four years.

Terry: Yes, and that must be about two hundred bottles of sherry ago.

June: Oh, she doesn't drink sherry all the time.

Terry: No, only when she's fit and well. When she's not feeling so good it's brandy. I tell you if she ever becomes a blood donor they could tap it straight off into the barrel.

June: She doesn't drink that much. You seem to forget she's nearly seventy-four.

Terry: Years old or per cent proof?

[*There is a knock at the door*]

Lucy: [*Outside*] It's only me.

Terry: [*Calling out*] We're closed.

June: Come in, dear.

Lucy: [*Entering*] I was just wondering if I could have that little piece of veal and ham pie that's in the larder.

June: Of course, dear. You must be famished after working so hard all day.

Lucy: Yes, I think perhaps I have overdone it a bit.

Terry: [*Looking as his bottle of sherry, and muttering to himself*] I'm sure you have.

Lucy: In fact I'm feeling a little bit faint.

Terry: [*Resigned*] Here we go again. [*He opens his cupboard and sees no brandy*] You're out of luck, dear. Look! There isn't any brandy.

Lucy: Yes there is, you've got nearly a full bottle.

Terry: Have I? [*He looks again*] Where?

Lucy: In my room. All I need is the glass.

2 Terry's and June's bedroom

It is later that night. **June** *is leaning back on the pillows contentedly.* **Terry** *is pottering around.*

June: You know, darling, that was one of the nicest meals we've ever had.

Terry: So it should be. Fourteen quid. And that's now. In five year's time it'll be more like thirty quid.

June: Why worry about what it's going to be *then*?

Terry: Because that's roughly the date we'll be eating out again.

Junt: Now just forget about it, and come to bed.

Terry: [*Getting into bed*] Right.

June: [*Mellow*] That wine was rather nice. I think I had a bit too much. [*Smiles at him*]

Terry: [*Getting into bed*] June, I've got to be up early in the morning. Good night, love.

June: Oh, don't go to sleep yet. I was looking forward to a little talk.

Terry: But we've been talking all evening.

June: Yes, darling, but not about this.

Terry: About what?

June: Oh – just a little thought.

Terry: Well, save it for the morning. G'night. [*He kisses her, turns his light out and settles down*]

[*Pause*]

June: Terry.

Terry: Not now.

June: But Terry. . . .

Terry: No, June.

June: All right, dear, doesn't matter. Some other time. I was only going to say, what about having a baby?

[*Pause*]

Terry: [*Sits up, puts the light on and stares at her*] Pardon?

June: A baby. Don't you think it would be nice?

Terry: Are you sure you didn't get a bang on the head today?

June: No.

Terry: You must be drunk then.

June: No, why should I be?

Terry: Well, barmy then. How can we possibly have a baby at your age?

June: Oh, Terry, I didn't mean *me*.

Terry: Oh. Well, I don't think I know anyone else well enough, do I?

June: I didn't actually mean have one – not that I still couldn't, mind you. I was talking about adopting one.

Terry: [*Blankly*] What for?

June: What do people usually adopt them for?

Terry: Because they haven't got any children of their own. We've got three.

June: Not at home. And I really miss them around the place. This has always been a family house and it should be ringing with the laughter of little children.

Terry: Blimey, how many do you want?

June: Well, only one . . . to begin with. Till we see how it goes.

Terry: I can't even get to sleep properly now, what's it going to be like when the place is ringing with laughter all night? No, June, I'm not going through all that again.

June: You never did. I was the one who had all the sleepless nights. You snored your way through it all.

Terry: I was keeping the bed warm for you.

June: Anyway, it doesn't have to be a baby. You can adopt someone of any age.

Terry: Right. We'll have a twenty-two year old Swedish blonde. I won't mind having a few sleepless nights then.

June: Now be serious. I really mean it. It would give us a new interest in life. Keep us young. Wouldn't you be happy to have someone to teach all about life, play with in the park, climb up on your knee?

Terry: Yes, the Swedish blonde. Now just forget all this re-awakening of your maternal instincts, and go to sleep. Here. [*He gives her his top pillow*] Cuddle that!

[**Terry** *turns his light out and lies down.* **June** *is left sitting there holding the pillow, lost in thought. After a pause she looks down at* **Terry**]

June: I think perhaps a boy would be rather nice.

Terry: [*Grabs the pillow back and wraps it round his ears and lies down*] No! No! No!

3   An office in the local borough council

June *and* **Terry** *are sitting at an empty desk, waiting to be interviewed. On the wall behind the desk there are 'Adoption' and 'Family Health' posters etc.* **Terry** *looks at his watch and gets up impatiently and paces up and down.*

Terry: How much longer do we have to wait?

June: Sit down, you'll wear a hole in the carpet.

Terry: They're lucky to have carpet. Who pays for it? We do. The rate-payers.

June: Don't let's get off on the wrong foot. First impressions are very important. They don't just hand children out to anyone.

Terry: Look, June, this is your idea not mine. I was quite happy to carry on with life the way it was. I mean, we've got enough problems with Lucy. So remember this is just a tentative enquiry.

June: Yes, dear. And thank you for being so understanding.

Terry: I don't know about that. I must be a simpleminded fool to listen to you. [*The door opens and an official enters unseen by* **Terry**. *His name is* **Mr Truscott**] Mad, that's what I am, stark raving mad.

[*The official looks somewhat startled*]

Mr Truscott: Oh dear.

Terry: [*Quickly bluffs his way out by pretending he's telling a joke*] . . .so the Irishman turned to the Scotsman and said. . . .

Mr Truscott: I'm awfully sorry to have kept you waiting.

Terry: [*Turns*] No he didn't say that, he said . . . oh, well, it doesn't matter now anyway. [*Apologetically*] I was just telling the wife a joke I heard in the pub. [**June** *gives him a surreptitious nudge*] What? Oh, in the public library, I mean.

Mr Truscott: Do sit down, Mr Fletcher.

Terry: Thank you.

[*They both sit down*]

Mr Truscott: How do you do? I'm Truscott.

Terry: Oh dear, that can be very painful. [*He chortles*]

Mr Truscott: [*Coldly*] Y-e-s. Well now, I have your letter here, Mrs Fletcher. It seems that you and your husband are both anxious to adopt.

June: Yes, that's right.

Mr Truscott: Well now, one has to consider certain aspects most carefully. Background, temperament, personality.

Terry: Quite right, we don't want any Tom, Dick or Harry.

Mr Truscott: Not the child's, yours.

Terry: Oh. Well, you haven't got any worries there. She's got plenty of background. County types, that lot. Very twin-set and pearls. Wouldn't talk to the likes of you and me.

June: Terry, for goodness' sake.

Terry: I'm only filling him in on your pedigree.

Mr Truscott: Yes, I'm sure it's very sound. What about you, Mr Fletcher?

Terry: Well, I think you better put me down as a sort of 'lovable mongrel'. Wouldn't quite make it at Crufts, but a damn good member of the tail-waggers' club.

Mr Truscott: This is a Child Adoption, not the Battersea Dogs' Home.

June: [*Looking at* **Terry**] We do realize that, Mr Truscott.

Mr Truscott: It does occur to me that this is a somewhat special case. Most of our enquiries tend to be from younger couples.

June: Yes, I suppose it does seem unusual at our time of life, but then we have had quite a bit of experience already, bringing up three children.

Mr Truscott: Were they your own?

Terry: [*Sarcastic*] No, we won 'em in a raffle. [*Serious*] Of course they were our own. A boy and two girls. Fine bunch of thoroughbreds, although I say it myself. I gave them the benefit of my knowledge. They didn't have to ask, I was always there, with guidance, suggestions and endless advice.

Mr Truscott: What happened?

June: They all left home.

Mr Truscott: Oh.

Terry: Well, you know what kids are like, they want to make their own way in the world. But we pointed them in the right direction, didn't we, dear?

June: I think so.

Mr Truscott: I see. And I suppose you're left with a vacuum in your house.

Terry: Oh yes, we've always had one of those, and a washing-machine. . . .

Mr Truscott: [*Cutting in*] No, no, I mean a void, an emptiness.

June: Yes, I suppose there is and I feel I'd like to - well - to become a. . . .

Mr Truscott: A mother again.

Terry: Yes. [*Then laughingly*] Not so much fun this way, but still. . . .

June: [*Quickly*] Is there anything else you need to know?

Mr Truscott: One or two things, yes. Er - age?

Terry: Not fussy. Anything from two upwards.

Mr Truscott: No, yours.

Terry: Well, I'm late forties and my wife is early.

Mr Truscott: We need to be more precise than that.

June: I'm forty-four.

Terry: I'm forty-seven, er – eight.

June: Nine.

Mr Truscott: Shall we close the bidding at forty-nine? [*He jots it down*]

Terry: But young at heart.

Mr Truscott: [*Makes a note*] Let's move on, shall we? What denomination are you?

June: C of E.

Terry: St Luke's. It's on the corner. Not a bad little church. The vicar does his best but he hasn't quite got the hang of a good sermon yet. He will keep trying to drag religion into it.

Mr Truscott: I'm sorry to have to ask this, but would you say that you were – how shall I put it – comfortable?

Terry: [*Looks at his chair*] Yes, it's all right.

Mr Truscott: Financially.

Terry: Oh, I see. Yes, I'm on a pretty good whack.

June: My husband's an Area Sales Manager. A very responsible position.

Mr Truscott: [*Mildly surprised*] Oh good. Well that's something in his favour. Well I can't hold out a great deal of hope that we can arrange anything right away.

June: Then we just have to wait, do we?

Mr Truscott: I'm afraid so, but in the meantime, may I make a suggestion? Having got some idea of what you're like, I think you could both be considered as proxy parents.

Terry: [*Rising*] How dare you. Come on, June, we don't have to sit here and be insul. . . .

June: No, Terry. *Proxy!*

Terry: Eh? Oh, proxy.

June: Just temporary, you mean, like foster parents? We could look after someone for just a little while.

Mr Truscott: Yes, we have numerous examples where the actual parents are away or indisposed. Mind you, in these cases, the youngsters do tend to be somewhat more grown-up.

Terry: [*Brightening up*] Good. Got any Swedish ones knocking about?

June: [*Ignoring him*] That sounds a very good idea, Mr Truscott. How do we go about it?

Mr Truscott: Leave it to me. I'll get you fixed up as soon as possible. [*He presses an intercom buzzer*] Would you come in please, Miss Swinton?

June: I feel sure my husband and I will enjoy the experience.

[*The door opens and in walks a very attractive young girl carrying a secretary's notebook*]

Terry: I'm damn sure I will. Is that her? She'll do.

June: Terry.

Terry: What? [*To the girl*] You'll love it at The Laurels. Got your things packed?

4   The Fletchers' kitchen

June, Lucy *and a 12-year-old, well-spoken schoolboy,*
Anthony Simpson, *are at the table. He is having tea.*

June: Another piece of cake, Anthony?

Anthony: No, thank you, Mrs Fletcher. I've had quite enough.

Lucy: Are you sure now? I made a nice big one specially for you.

Anthony: No, really, I couldn't. But it was absolutely super.

June: Some more tea?

Anthony: Yes, please.

June: [*Pouring*] My own children always used to come home starving. I don't suppose school meals have changed much.

Anthony: They're not too bad.

June: You must let me know the things you don't like so we can avoid them during your month's stay here.

Anthony: Oh, I'm not fussy. I like everything.

Lucy: What a good boy. I should keep him and get rid of Terry.

June: [*Laughs*] Yes.

Lucy: Does your father have to make these business trips very often?

Anthony: Yes, but this is the first time Mum's had to go as well.

Lucy: Do you get a lot of homework?

Anthony: I've got three subjects tonight. Do you

think Mr Fletcher would know anything about England in the 1600s?

June: I doubt it. He's not all that good on the 1970s.

Terry: [*In the hall*] June?

June: Hello . . . here comes Mastermind now. [*Calls*] I'm here, darling. Come and meet Anthony.

Terry: [*Entering*] Ah. So this is our young friend.

June: Yes. . . . Anthony Simpson.

Anthony: [*Stands up*] How do you do, sir?

June: This is Anthony Simpson.

Terry: Hello, Tony, I'm Terry. Looking after you all right, are they?

June: Yes, he's just had his tea.

Lucy: And I made the cake.

Terry: [*To* **Anthony**] Got a good doctor, have you?

Lucy: It was very nice, wasn't it, Anthony?

Anthony: Yes, thank you.

June: [*To* **Terry**, *nostalgically*] It's quite like the old days, isn't it, having family tea in the kitchen?

Terry: Yes, I suppose it is. This could be Frank all over again. He was a fine looking lad too. Many's the time he sat at that table doing his homework. And I was there if he ever needed any help. The same goes for you Anthony. Anything you want to know, you've only got to ask.

Anthony: Thank you, sir. I've got quite a lot to do tonight. I've got to write an essay on the Great Plague of London.

Terry: I should know about that. She's been staying with us for the last four years. [*He laughs*]

Lucy: Now don't teach him any of your bad habits, Terry.

Anthony: Oh, and maybe you might remember something about Pythagoras?

Terry: Oh, yes, that rings a bell. [*To* **June**] One of the Greek islands, isn't it, June? Not much I don't know about geography.

Anthony: It's geometry, sir.

Terry: What? Oh, *that* Pythagoras, yes. The sum of the whatsits on the hypothesis are equal to the sum of two thingummys on the other side of the how's-your-father.

June: How are you doing at school, Anthony?

Anthony: Not bad, at the moment I'm about third in the class. [*He gathers up his books*]

June: Jolly good. And if you want to stay there I should do your own homework. [*To* **Terry**] You never got anywhere near your School Cert., did you?

Terry: Oh, yes, I did. She was always taking me round the back of the pavilion. [*He laughs*] Come on, Tony, let's go into the sitting room and leave Matron to get on with dinner. [*He puts a fatherly arm round the boy*]

Terry: Get plenty of cricket, do you?

Anthony: Yes.

Terry: That's the game. I remember on one occasion I was getting on for seventy, and. . . .

June: Well, it won't be long before you're there again, dear.

Terry: [*He gives her a look and goes out with* **Anthony**] Thank you.

Lucy: He seems a nice young lad. I'm sure he'll get on well with Terry.

June: I hope so. You don't think it was a bit soon to introduce the new boy to Flashman. . . ? [*They both laugh*]

5   The Fletchers' sitting room

Anthony *is sitting down on the sofa listening to* **Terry** *who is standing by the mantelpiece continuing his cricket saga.*

Terry: . . . Mark you, by this time the light was beginning to go. I could have appealed but we needed two to win. I could hardly see that last ball. It came out of the gloom like a thunderbolt. Dennis Lillee wasn't in it. Lethal it was, head height. So what did I do? Hooked it for four and the match was ours. But it was a close thing.

Anthony: Gosh, you were lucky. Just think how you'd have felt if the girls had won.

Terry: Well, that's cricket for you. Still, this won't get your homework done, will it? Got much to do?

Anthony: Yes, I'd better get on with it, if you don't mind.

Terry: No, you carry on. [*He goes for a drink*] Forget I'm here. Just going to have a drink. Then when you've finished, we'll have a game of something. D'you like snakes and ladders?

Anthony: I prefer chess.

Terry: Oh, well – it's all the same to me.

[**Anthony** *starts his work and* **Terry** *whistles as he*

pours himself a drink. **Anthony** *gives him a slight
look.* **Terry** *turns, and as he walks back to the
mantelpiece he stops and glances over the boy's
shoulder. The boy ignores him and carries on doing
his work.* **Terry** *grunts approvingly*]

Terry: Mm - uh - uh - mm - Yes, your first three are
right. Keep it up. [*He goes and sits down*] Dear old
vulgar fractions ... square roots ... algebra ... how it
all comes flooding back. Prentice, he was the maths
master - old Tweaky Prentice. We used to call him
that because, if you made a mistake, he'd grab a
handful of your hair and give it a tweak. [*Chuckling*]
All bald we were in the Fifth Form. And then there
was old Toothy Tatlock, the games master, we gave
him a hard time. What pranks we got up to! I
remember once we put itching powder in his rugger
shorts. He was leaping about like a grasshopper. [*He
laughs*] Happy days. Sometimes I think you kids miss
a lot of fun. You see when I was. . . .

Anthony: Er - excuse me, Mr Fletcher.

Terry: Yes?

Anthony: Would you rather I did my homework
upstairs?

Terry: Why? What's the problem?

Anthony: Well, I am finding it rather difficult to. . . .

Terry: [*Getting up*] Oh, there's always one you get
stuck on. [*Going over to him*] Which one is it? Show
me which one are you on.

Anthony: Well, I'm still on number four.

Terry: [*Picking up the book*] It takes four men eight
days to dig. . . .

June: [*Enters with a screw-top jar*] Darling, could you just open this for me?

Terry: Ssh, not now, we're doing homework.

June: I told you to leave him alone.

Terry: He needs help, June. Anybody would need help with this.

June: Including you, darling?

Terry: Yes, listen. It takes four men eight days to dig a ditch a hundred metres long, one metre deep and one and a half metres wide and then fill it with water at the rate of five litres an hour. How long would it take if there were only three men? That's four over eight. . . . No, five divided by one and a half – [*He turns to the cover of the book*] Who writes this rubbish? Professor A. C. Potts. That's the sort of twaddle they're filling their heads with. Now I ask you, does it make sense?

June: I don't know. Does it, Anthony?

Anthony: Yes, I think so.

Terry: [*Giving the book back*] Well, you do it.

Anthony: Thanks.

June: [*Blandly*] Open this, darling.

Terry: [*Takes the jar and tries to open it*] It's not realistic. What good's that to a bright young boy like Anthony? I mean, when he leaves school, he's not going to spend his life digging ditches and filling them with water. [*He is struggling with the jar*]

June: That's not the point, Terry. These are exercises for the mind. Teaching them how to approach a problem.

Terry: Yes, but I'd like to see them taught more

practical things. Real-life problems. Like how to get the top off a stubborn jar.

June: [*Taking the jar back*] I'll do it myself.

Anthony: Can I help?

Terry: No, old lad, you've got enough to do already. [*To* **June**] Poor boy, he's got the plague, Pythagoras and Professor Potts, all in one night. That's going to stand him in good stead for the future. Great social asset he'll be at any party. "What a delightful house this is. I do believe it's equal to twice the size of the two houses on the other side of the square.... Keeping free of the plague, are you? . . .Love your swimming-pool, it must have taken four men at least eight days to build it. . . ."

June: Never mind, Anthony. At least I can help you with one of your problems tonight.

Anthony: Could you really?

June: Yes. I'll lock him in the kitchen. [*Grabbing* **Terry**] Come on.

Terry: All right, all right. [*Over his shoulder*] I'll be out to play later.

6 The Fletchers' sitting room

Later that evening, **Terry** *and* **Anthony** *are seated, either side of a chessboard.* **Anthony** *is reading a comic while* **Terry** *is considering his next move with great deliberation. He goes to make a move but thinks better of it. He has another look, then with a sudden flash of inspiration he moves a piece.*

Terry: Your move.

Anthony: [*Glancing up from his comic and making a move*] Checkmate.

7 A cricket field

Terry *is batting.* **June** *is wicket-keeping. The ball comes to* **Terry.** *He plays a stroke, misses and the ball hits the wicket.*

June: Howzat!

Terry: [*Firmly*] I wasn't ready. Take it again. [*Pause.* **Terry** *faces another delivery. He plays a stroke outside the off stump and misses.* **June** *catches it*]

June: Howzat!

Terry: I never touched it.

[*A third delivery pitches short.* **Terry** *steps out of his crease, swipes and misses.* **June** *stumps him*]

June: Out.

Terry: [*Hastily*] I was miles in.

[*A fourth ball is delivered.* **Terry** *is clean bowled*]

June: [*Sarcastically*] Nearly had you that time.

Terry: All right. [*Calling up the pitch*] That's enough, Lucy. Let Tony bowl now.

8 The Fletchers' sitting room

Terry *and* **Anthony** *are at the table, playing Monopoly.*

Terry: One thing I can teach you, Tony, is simple economics. Remember, if your capital expenditure doesn't justify the return, in terms of potential income, then that can only lead to bankruptcy and financial ruin.

Anthony:　Well, you shouldn't put all those hotels on Park Lane and Mayfair and Bond Street.

9　The golf course

Terry *and* **June** *are watching* **Anthony** *who is shaping up for a drive.*

Terry:　No, not like that, Tony.

June:　Don't be too hard on him, he's never played before.

Terry:　I only want to help. After all, this is my game. [*To* **Anthony**] Keep your head down, left arm straight, and a nice easy swing and don't forget to follow through.

Anthony:　It's a lot to remember.

June:　I shouldn't worry, go on, just hit it. [*Anthony drives off. They watch the flight of the ball. The ball lands on the green a few yards from the pin*] Good shot.

[*Pause*]

Terry:　Now, let me just show you where you're going wrong.

10　The road outside the Fletchers' house

Anthony *is sitting in the back of a car with the window wound down. He is waving through it. The car, with his parents in the front, drives off.* **Terry**, **June** *and* **Lucy** *wave them off from the pavement.*

11 Terry's and June's bedroom

It is bed time. **June** *is sitting up in bed,* **Terry** *has his dressing gown and pyjama jacket on and is folding his trousers and putting them over a chair.*

Terry: Quite a nice lad, really. We got on famously.

June: Yes, I enjoyed having him, and he was no trouble. Can we do it again sometime?

Terry: Don't see why not, if they're all like him. Bit studious, perhaps, but well behaved. Didn't get up to much mischief. [*He chuckles*] Not like me at his age. [*He starts to put on his pyjama trousers under his dressing gown*]

June: I think it's done you good, too. You're looking ten years younger.

Terry: [*Removing his dressing gown*] Well, I've always got on well with kids. They do keep you up to scratch and I like to think that maybe he's learnt something from me. [*He starts scratching himself vaguely*] It was worth it, even if it was just one little thing I said that he's taken notice of. [*He scratches more urgently*]

June: What's the matter?

Terry: I seem to be itching all over. . . . I can't understand – [*Suddenly he realizes*] June!

June: What?

Terry: [*Jumping around and tearing off his pyjama jacket*] He *did* remember something I said! The little blighter – ow – ow!

The end

Rising Damp

Great Expectations

Eric Chappell

Produced by Yorkshire Television and first shown on ITV on 18 April 1978

Characters

Rigsby, a landlord of a seedy lodging house
Ruth Jones, one of his tenants
Philip, another tenant, the son of an African chieftain
Veronica, Rigsby's wife (they have separated)
Snell, a solicitor
Maud, Rigsby's aunt

Rigsby (Leonard Rossiter) and Ruth (Frances de la Tour) prepare for Aunt Maud's visit, in the series Rising Damp, *produced by* ⋎ *Yorkshire Television. Photograph © Trident Television Ltd 1977*

Great Expectations

1   Philip's attic flat in Rigsby's lodging house

It is morning. **Philip** *is reading.* **Rigsby** *enters the room backwards, casting nervous glances around the door.*

Philip: [*Mystified*] What's the matter, Rigsby?

Rigsby: Shush!

Philip: Rigsby, I'm busy. I don't want you coming up here. And it's no use walking in backwards – I know you're not just leaving.

Rigsby: Shush! I'm not visiting – I'm avoiding someone. I think he's from the Council – there's something sinister about him.

Philip: What makes you think that?

Rigsby: I know the type. He's got those hunched shoulders from crouching over figures all day, and those long bony fingers you get from squeezing blood out of a stone.

Philip: Well, why should that worry you, Rigsby? Unless you're hiding something.

Rigsby: Listen, I've got nothing to hide. My conscience is clear, don't you worry. [*He picks up a* *washing leather*] If he asks for me – I'm the window cleaner.

Philip: I thought you'd got nothing to hide?

Rigsby: I haven't. But that doesn't stop them persecuting you. Once they know you've put a bit of money away for your old age they can't wait to get their thieving hands on it. Coming around here with their rate demands. You've only got to look at his face to see he's absolutely ruthless.

Philip: [*Smiles*] Haven't you paid your rates, Rigsby?

Rigsby: [*Fiercely*] Who said I hadn't paid my rates? Who told you that? You watch your tongue. I'm in dispute. I'm over-assessed. I'm a poor man. [*The door opens*] I'm the window cleaner. [*He starts cleaning the window.* **Snell** *enters. He is wearing a dark jacket and pin-stripe trousers and is carrying a briefcase*]

Snell: Excuse me, my name's Snell.

Rigsby: [*Shrugs*] We've all got problems.

Philip: Can I help you?

Snell: I'm looking for Mr Rigsby.

Rigsby: You've just missed him. Leave your card and we'll tell him you called.

Snell: Oh, I don't think I have a card.

Rigsby: No card. You could be anyone. [*To* **Philip**] Keep your eye on the silver. [*He returns to cleaning the window*]

Philip: What do you want Mr Rigsby for?

Snell: It's a personal matter.

Philip: You can tell us – we're his friends.

Snell: [*Hesitates*] Oh, I can't really tell his friends. You see it's strictly confidential. It must be kept within a very small circle.

Philip: His friends are a very small circle.

[**Rigsby** *scowls*]

Snell: I'm sorry but it's of a financial nature –

Rigsby: I thought so. And you've just dropped in for a little chat. What have you got in the bag – your thumb-screws?

Snell: I beg your pardon?

Rigsby: I don't know why you can't leave him alone. Persecuting an old soldier like this. A man who left his health and strength on the beach at Dunkirk.

Snell: I really don't think there's any need for all this –

Rigsby: And what are you doing about the rats? You tell me that.

Snell: [*Nervously*] Rats?

Rigsby: They're getting bolder everyday. You ask him across the road with the wooden leg. Sitting there reading his Sunday paper, heard this gnawing sound, stood up and collapsed in a pile of sawdust. And what are the Council doing? Nothing. [*He returns to window cleaning*]

Snell: I think there's some misunderstanding. I'm not from the Council. I'm from Hargreaves the Solicitors. And since you insist on knowing, I've come to see Mr Rigsby regarding the estate of his late uncle – George Rigsby.

Philip: You mean he's been left something?

[**Rigsby** *stops cleaning*]

Snell: Yes, he gets the residue of the estate.

[**Rigsby**'s *mouth drops open*]

Philip: Is it much?

Snell: A considerable sum.

Philip: What would you call a considerable sum?

[**Rigsby** *strains to overhear*]

Snell: A figure not unadjacent to £50,000.

Philip: That's a considerable sum.

Snell: Yes, I hope it won't be too much of a shock for Mr Rigsby.

Rigsby: [*Letting out a triumphant roar and capering around the room*] Rigsby's in the money. He's got the residue. Did you hear that? He's got the residue, as the parrot said when he sat on the vicar's shoulder. [*He opens the door and shouts down the stairs*] Did you hear that? Rigsby's got the residue.

Snell: [*Staring at* **Philip**] My goodness, if it has this effect on the window cleaner, what's it going to do to Mr Rigsby?

Rigsby: [*Returns. He drags* **Snell** *to his feet and waltzes him around the room*] I was wrong about you. You've got a very nice face. I never knew the old devil had any money. Hadn't heard of him in years.

Snell: [*Angrily*] Stop!

Rigsby: [*Stops dancing.* **Snell** *disengages himself*] What's the matter? Don't you like the waltz?

Snell: [*Coldly*] Mr Rigsby - I presume?

Rigsby: Yes - how did you guess?

Snell: I think it was your very natural display of grief on hearing of your uncle's death.

Rigsby: Oh. Well, of course, I'm very sorry. Mind you, I hadn't seen him in years. [*Sadly*] Poor old Uncle George, I hope it was a peaceful end. To think he thought of me at the last when I'd almost forgotten him. Life can be cruel. Do you know what I'm going to do? I'm going to throw myself on that man's grave and beg his forgiveness.

Snell: I wouldn't advise that, Mr Rigsby – we've just scattered his ashes on the Mersey. I'll leave you with the necessary papers. Perhaps when you've recovered from your grief you'll call at the office and advise us on how we should deal with the money.

Rigsby: You just bundle it into fivers – I'll do the rest. And since you brought the good news. . . .

Snell: Yes?

Rigsby: Here's something for your bus fare.

Snell: [*Angrily*] Thank you. Your generosity over-whelms me, Mr Risgby. Good day. [*He leaves*]

Philip: Congratulations, Rigsby. This calls for a celebration. Sit down – have a drink.

Rigsby: Oh, yes? It's starting already, is it?

Philip: What do you mean?

Rigsby: 'Sit down – have a drink.' You've certainly changed your attitude. It wouldn't have anything to do with the money, would it?

Philip: [*Angrily*] Certainly not. Rigsby, if you think I'm after your money. . . .

Rigsby: No, I'm sorry – I shouldn't have said that. I suppose it's suddenly being rich. Do you realize? I'm rich. Rich, rich, rich. But I've got to be careful. Once they get to know they'll all be round.

Philip: Who will?

Rigsby: The fortune hunters, the fast women, the double-glazing people. they'll all be after my money. But they won't get it – not a penny. I've waited too long for this.

Philip: You'd better watch it, Rigsby. If the money's going to make you miserable. . . .

Rigsby: You don't understand. It's no fun being rich. It can bring a lot of worry. I mean, what am I going to do about the begging letters?

Philip: Oh, I shouldn't worry, Rigsby. I'd keep writing them.

Rigsby: Yes, that's what I – [*Stops, scowls*] Right, that's one less for the champagne reception. [*He leaves*]

2   Rigsby's own room

It is now two days later. **Rigsby** *is wearing his best suit and smoking a cigar. He hums cheerfully as he brushes himself down in the mirror.*

Rigsby: That cat's hairs get everywhere. [*To the cat*] If you don't stop moulting I'll give you a coat of varnish. And don't look like that – no one's indispensable. You could find yourself replaced by a Blue Persian – something more in keeping with my status.

[**Ruth** *enters carrying* Home and Garden *magazine*]

Ruth: Good morning, Mr Rigsby. My word, we do look smart this morning – so distinguished.

Rigsby: [*Hiding a knowing smile*] Do you think so,

Miss Jones? I take it you've heard about my good fortune.

Ruth: Oh yes. And I must say it couldn't have happened to a nicer person.

Rigsby: I quite agree. Now, if you'll excuse me. I haven't much time for chit-chat this morning. I have an appointment with my tailor.

Ruth: Oh, I thought you always went to that man on the market – the one by the hotdog stall?

Rigsby: [*Indignantly*] Miss Jones, I'm having a bespoke hacking jacket and cavalry twills, a yellow waistcoat and a tie with foxes' heads on it. If you think I'm going to get them from some herbert who stands by the hotdog stall, you're mistaken. Besides, everything from there smells of onions.

Ruth: Well, I must say it's very exciting, seeing you rise in the world like this.

Rigsby: [*Patiently*] I'm not rising in the world, Miss Jones. I've already risen. It's just that now I can enjoy the little luxuries in keeping with my status. Well, time presses and I've also got to see my accountant at eleven for a chat about Capital Gains.

Ruth: I can see you're a very busy man, Mr Rigsby. I don't suppose you have any time for me now?

Rigsby: Nonsense, Miss Jones. I've always got time for you. [*Glances at his watch*] I can give you five minutes.

Ruth: [*Hesitantly*] I was wondering, since you've had this windfall, if I could have a new carpet for my room.

Rigsby: [*Frowns*] A new carpet, Miss Jones? What's wrong with the coconut matting?

Ruth: Nothing, it's very nice, but it does make these red rings on my knees. I thought if I had something like this. . . . [*Shows him a picture in a magazine*] Tufty pile, wall to wall. . . .

Rigsby: [*Studies the picture coldly*] You mean this one - with the young couple lying across it in their underwear?

Ruth: Er . . . yes.

Rigsby: Well, you certainly couldn't do that on coconut matting. You'd get red rings everywhere. Are you planning to do this sort of thing, Miss Jones?

Ruth: Certainly not - I'd just like a little more comfort.

Rigsby: You don't want a thick carpet, Miss Jones. They're full of static electricity. Very dangerous. Why do you think they're sprawled out like that? Probably been electrocuted.

Ruth: But, Mr Rigsby. . . .

Rigsby: Besides, if I let you have a fitted carpet they'd all want one.

Ruth: But, Mr Rigsby. . . . [*Fondles his tie*] I always thought I was just a little bit special.

Rigsby: Don't wheedle, Miss Jones. I know I've paid you some attention in the past but that was when I had more time. [*Sighs*] Women just won't leave me alone these days.

Ruth: [*Coldly*] Really?

Rigsby: That woman who owns the wet fish stand's been making eyes at me again. I think she fancies me.

Ruth: Perhaps she's looking for stock?

Rigsby: [*Indignantly*] What do you mean? She's after

me. She took so long counting out the change yesterday the coins still smell of haddock.

Ruth: She's probably heard about the money.

Rigsby: Well, I don't deny that money plus good looks can be a pretty explosive combination. But I think her feelings are genuine. [*Smirks*] She said she thought I was cracking.

Ruth: Oh really, where? [*She crosses angrily to the door*]

Rigsby: What's the matter, Miss Jones?

Ruth: I'm going. I don't want you to think I'm after your money, Mr Rigsby. [*She goes out*]

Rigsby: Just as I thought. Envy. She's being eaten away by it.

Philip: [*Entering with a brochure*] What's the matter with Ruth?

Rigsby: A woman scorned, I'm afraid. Well, you know how it is. I'm moving in different circles these days. I'm already down for the golf club. I'll be playing with all those divorcees in ankle socks, twin sets and matching pearls. I'll be mingling with the camel-haired coat brigade. They'll probably invite me over for a rubber of bridge, and then I'll be away. You can get a lot of footsy in under those bridge tables.

Philip: Er . . . Rigsby.

Rigsby: Well, what is it?

Philip: I was thinking. Now you've got some money. What about a heated towel rail for the bathroom?

Rigsby: [*Coldly*] A what?

Philip: A heated towel rail.

Rigsby: You're not getting a heated towel rail. You

spend long enough in that bathroom as it is. You won't be satisfied until it's like Equatorial Africa in there.

Philip: But you can afford it.

Rigsby: Yes, but where's it going to end? Let me see. [*He studies the brochure*] Just look at this. 'Matching suite in aztec gold – hand painted mosaic tiles – seascape carpet in aquamarine – sepia tinted mirror.' [*He stops and stares*] Sepia tinted mirror! What do you want with a sepia tinted mirror? You'd never see yourself. You know your trouble, you're getting soft.

Philip: You're just too mean to spend money, Rigsby. All I wanted was a towel rail.

Rigsby: What's the matter? Have you burned your bum on the paraffin stove again?

[**Snell** *enters*]

Rigsby: [*Brightens*] Ah, Mr Snell. Has the money come through yet?

Snell: [*Suppressing a smile*] No, Mr Rigsby – I'm afraid there's been a complication.

Rigsby: Don't tell me it was all a mistake. I couldn't bear it.

Snell: No, there was simply a condition I should have mentioned, a formality, the fine print. [*He bites his knuckle*]

Rigsby: Ah, the fine print – as long as it's nothing serious.

Snell: [*Still concealing mirth*] As you know, George Rigsby was a happily married man.

Rigsby: I know – his wife had been dead for years.

Snell: Still, he had fond memories – and he'd lived to see the marriages of his close relatives founder on the roots of acrimony and discord.

Rigsby: Yes, most distressing.

Snell: And that's the condition. That you should be happily married.

Rigsby: What!

Snell: Your Aunt Maud, one of the executors, is coming tomorrow to ensure that this condition is fulfilled. Then we can release the money.

Rigsby: Aunt Maud! That old bat! But she hates me.

Snell: [*Beams*] Does she really? Still, I'm sure you'll have no difficulty in satisfying her. [*Titters*] You're clearly a man of great personal charm. And you are married?

Rigsby: Oh yes.

Snell: Your wife must consider herself the most fortunate of women. Good day, Mr Rigsby. [*He goes out, and we hear him laugh once he is out of the room*]

Rigsby: Did you hear that? I was right about him. He's sadistic. [**Philip** *screws the brochure into a ball*] What are you doing?

Philip: Well, we can forget the money now.

Rigsby: That's what you think. I'm not losing that money – not now. I've waited too long. It's all right for Uncle George, he only saw my wife at the wedding. She was all sweetness and light then – except when she belted me one for standing on the train of her dress. He never saw her again – none of them did. [*He stops*] That's it. Aunt Maud won't remember her. All I've got to do is get someone to take her place. [*He looks thoughtfully at the ceiling*]

Philip: You don't mean. . . ? She wouldn't do it.

Rigsby: [*Smiles*] Everyone's got their price. [*He goes out*]

3   Ruth's room

Ruth *and* **Rigsby** *are talking.*

Ruth: [*Horrified*] You mean you want me to impersonate your wife, Mr Rigsby?

Rigsby: Only for a few hours, Miss Jones.

Ruth: I couldn't, it would be wrong, it would be illegal. You're supposed to be happily married.

Rigsby: I am happily married – it's just that she lives in Cleethorpes and I live here.

Ruth: [*Firmly*] No, I'm sorry. I couldn't do it – and it's no use trying to persuade me.

Rigsby: [*He smiles, opens a magazine, and reads*] 'Sink your feet into the velvet luxury of our deep pile – enjoy the sensual pleasure of our delicate fibres – choose from our rich autumnal shades.'

Ruth: What do I have to do?

Rigsby: Just play the affectionate spouse, Miss Jones. I've got some of her old clothes down there.

Ruth: You can't keep calling me Miss Jones. What was her name?

Rigsby: Veronica.

Ruth: Veronica. [*Grimaces*] I knew there'd be sacrifices. What was she like, Mr Rigsby?

Rigsby: What was she like? Well, actually she's very difficult to describe. The word evades me at the moment.

Ruth: You must remember what she was like, Mr Rigsby. Don't be horrible.

Rigsby: That's the word – horrible.

Ruth: Did she have any traits they may remember?

Rigsby: Well, she had this very individual way with a cigarette – she kept it in her mouth while she talked. I don't know if they'll remember that – she did take it out during the service. And then of course there was the bronchial cough – she was always on high tar, you see.

Ruth: I don't know if I could manage that, Mr Rigsby.

Rigsby: And then there was the distinctive laugh.

Ruth: What was it like?

Rigsby: Well, it was a sort of cross between a pneumatic drill and someone shooting crows.

Ruth: I certainly couldn't do that.

Rigsby: I didn't say it would, Miss Jones - not for a woman of your refinement. You see she did have this robust cockney sense of humour – always ready for a quick knees up. And she did have this habit of slapping you on the back to emphasize a point – she almost put the vicar through the vestry wall. Of course that was when she was in a good mood – if she was piqued she'd hit you with her handbag.

Ruth: [*Horrified*] No, I can't possibly do it. My whole nature would rebel.

Rigsby: [*He hands her a cigarette*] Just give it a whirl, Miss Jones.

Ruth: Very well. [*She lights the cigarette*] Are you ready? 'Cor! Luv a duck! [*She inhales greedily and collapses in a fit of coughing*]

Rigsby: [*Patting her on the back*] You've got the cough, Miss Jones.

4   Rigsby's room

Rigsby *is alone.* **Philip** *enters.*

Philip: Well, what did she say?

Rigsby: She's not very happy about it.

Philip: [*Triumphantly*] I told you. 'Everyone has his price.' Well, not Ruth. I know her. She's got integrity. She's too decent – too honest. . . .

[**Ruth** *enters from the bedroom. She is dressed in a 1946-style suit and carries a shoulder bag. She has a cigarette in her mouth*]

Philip: [*Shocked*] Ruth! How could you?

Ruth: [*In a cockney accent*] What do you mean, cock? I'd do anything to sink my plates into a soft, velvet pile. Stone the crows – I've gorn out. Give me a light, my old china.

5   Rigsby's room

It is the next afternoon. **Ruth** *is setting the table.* **Rigsby** *is preparing to go out.*

Rigsby: How do I look, Miss Jones?

Ruth: Don't you mean Veronica?

Ruth: Yes, of course – how do I look, Veronica?

Ruth: Very nice, Mr Rigsby. [*Frowns*] I can't call you that. What is your first name?

Rigsby: [*Awkwardly*] Well, I don't think we need to go to those lengths, I. . . .

Ruth: Mr Rigsby, we are supposed to be married. What did she call you?

Rigsby: Almost everything.

Ruth: I mean at the beginning – when she was being affectionate.

Rigsby: Well, we didn't go in for endearments – not even in the early days. She'd just smile gently, put her hand on mine and say, 'Now then, ratbag.'

Ruth: I can't call you that. What is your name?

Rigsby: Rupert.

Ruth: What?

Rigsby: Rupert.

Ruth: Rupert! [*She stifles her laughter*] I'm sorry, Mr Rigsby – only you don't look like a Rupert.

Rigsby: [*Indignantly*] Of course, I don't look like a Rupert. He's a little woolly bear with check trousers and a scarf. I stopped using it. They always used to say 'Oh yes, and where's Bill Badger?'

Ruth: Well, I shan't. I think it's a nice name. Now what should I get Aunt Maud for her tea? What about some hot buttered scones?

Rigsby: I don't think so, Miss Jones. I think you'd be courting disaster with her teeth. Besides, she's a martyr to wind and we don't want any social embarrassment. It'd better be something she can dip. Well, I'd better get off. The train should be in by now – unless she's arrived by broom. [*He crosses to the door. Hesitates*] I was thinking. Perhaps we ought to slip into the part now. What about a kiss before I go?

Ruth: I beg your pardon?

Rigsby: A kiss. After all, you've got to start acting like a wife.

Ruth: I don't think there's any need for that sort of thing. [*After a pause she gives him a peck on the cheek*]

Rigsby: That's very good, Miss Jones. Only I was thinking of something a little more affectionate. I am going out in the busy traffic. I could have an accident. I could be stretched out in the gutter motionless. What would be your first reaction?

Ruth: Are you wearing clean underwear?

Rigsby: That's not very affectionate. We're supposed to be a loving couple.

Ruth: [*Sighs*] Very well, Mr Rigsby – I mean, Rupert.

[*They kiss clumsily but tenderly, then look embarrassed for a moment*]

Rigsby: [*Sighs*] I can't help thinking of what might have been – if fate had been kinder. If our paths had crossed earlier. Where were you, Miss Jones, when I was young and free?

Ruth: In my pram, I should think.

Rigsby: It wasn't to be, was it? And now it's too late.

Ruth: [*Quietly*] Is it? They say it's never too late – isn't that what they say?

Rigsby: Yes, well, what I say – [*Stops*] What! [*Suspiciously*] You've never said that before, Miss Jones. A new warmth seems to have entered our relationship all of a sudden.

Ruth: [*Coldly*] Don't look so worried, Mr Rigsby – I'm not after your money.

Rigsby: Miss Jones. . . .

Ruth: Please! Veronica, remember! Cripes! Look at the gin and lime. You'd better get into the old jam-jar and whistle down to the station. Can't keep the old bat waiting – she'll have the abb-dabs. [*She pushes* **Rigsby** *out*]

6 The hallway

It is a little later. **Philip** *enters the hall at the same time as does* **Veronica Rigsby**. *She is a well made woman but not as gigantic or grotesque as* **Rigsby** *has described.*

Veronica: Hello, sunshine. Is he in?

Philip: Who?

Veronica: Captain Bligh. The old skinflint – or perhaps I shouldn't say that now he's come into money.

Philip: Oh, you mean Rigsby. That's his room – there.

Veronica: Ta. Are you staying here?

Philip: Yes.

Veronica: Well, watch him. [*She gives her celebrated laugh and slaps* **Philip** *on the shoulder*]

Philip: You must be Aunt Maud. [*He rubs his shoulder*]

Veronica: Stone me! Do I look that old? That comes from being married to him. I was a beautiful girl before he got 'old of me. Of course it was years ago now but I still wake up screaming. . . . [*Laughs*]

Philip: I don't understand. . . . Who are you?

Veronica: I'm Mrs Rigsby. Come back to rattle my chains.

[*She goes out laughing.* **Philip**'s *amazement breaks into a slow smile*]

7   Rigsby's room

Veronica *enters.* **Ruth** *gives her a welcoming smile.*

Ruth: Hello, dearie. Just in time for a cup of char – or would you prefer a drop of mother's ruin? [*Laughs*]

Veronica: [*She stares*] I'm looking for Mr Rigsby.

Ruth: You must have just missed him. Never mind, all girls together. Park your b-t-m in that chair and get stuck in. And don't worry about the wind. I suffer from it something chronic – just loosen your stays, gel, and have a good nosh. We'll all be old one day.

Veronica: I'm not hungry.

Ruth: Oh. Would you like a fag? [**Veronica** *takes a cigarette*] That's right. The doctor says they'll be the blooming death of me. But I don't care. You only live once, ain't that right, Maud?

Veronica: [*Coldly*] Who are you? I don't think I've had the pleasure.

Ruth: Haven't you? Must be your age. [*Laughs*] Don't you know me? Veronica.

Veronica: You've changed.

Ruth: Were you at the wedding?

Veronica: I thought I was – now I'm beginning to wonder.

Ruth: I'm not surprised. What a day. And when old Rupert fell down in the aisle – laugh – I nearly bust me girdle.

Veronica: And you're still together? I never thought it would last.

Ruth: You mean because I hit him with me bouquet? Well, he trod on me blooming train, didn't he? Clumsy burk. Still, he's not been too bad, Maud – I mustn't grumble.

Veronica: Yes, now, where did you go for your honeymoon?

Ruth: Where did we go for our honeymoon? You might well ask. [*She laughs*] Where did we go for our honeymoon. . . .

Veronica: Well, where was it?

Ruth: It was Southend, wasn't it?

Veronica: I thought it was Blackpool.

Ruth: Southend the first week – Blackpool the second. But to tell the truth, by the second week I was past caring! [*She laughs again*] Know what I mean, Maud?

Veronica: I can't get over how young you look.

Ruth: Love of a good man, Maud.

Veronica: Have you got a photograph of the wedding?

Ruth: No. It was a slosh-up, Maud. All those groups, all that posing, standing there in the rain – no film in the camera. . . .

Veronica: That's funny. I've got one.

Ruth: What? [**Veronica** *produces a picture*] My Gawd! Don't I look a fright. And look at Rupert. Who's holding him up? Glassy-eyed and legless. He looks like the condemned man. My, we've certainly changed.

Veronica: [*Icily*] You certainly have - you're six inches taller.

Ruth: No, that's the low archway - I had to crouch or I'd have banged my bonce on it.

Veronica: And you've been together all these years. That's surprising considering he never had a proper job.

Ruth: Well, he had this back trouble, didn't he? Couldn't get it off the flaming bed. [*She laughs and slaps* **Veronica** *on the shoulder*] But he's a different man these days. He's not the person you once knew.

Veronica: He's not the only one.

Ruth: What?

Veronica: You're not Veronica.

Ruth: [*Is crestfallen and drops the pretence*] How did you know? It was the picture, I suppose. I don't know why I agreed to do it. She sounds a terrible woman.

Veronica: Oh. What's he been saying?

Ruth: [*Confidentially*] You don't know the half, Maud. Led him a dog's life.

Veronica: [*Grimly*] She did, did she?

Ruth: Oh yus - I mean yes. Always drawing on a cigarette - he couldn't see her for smoke some nights. And then there was the laugh.

Veronica: What sort of laugh?

Ruth: [*Giggles*] Mr Rigsby said it was a cross between a pneumatic drill and someone shooting crows. I think she must have been a bit common. I only did it so that Mr Rigsby would get the money. He had to prove he was happily married. Happily married! To that woman. Well, I'm glad you found out - I'm glad the pretence is over.

Veronica: Oh, I knew you couldn't be his wife.

Ruth: Why?

Veronica: Because I am.

Ruth: [*Stares*] What! Oh! [*She rises*] Stone the crows! [*She goes out hurriedly.* **Veronica** *laughs*]

8 The hallway

Rigsby *is closing the front door behind a grim-faced* **Aunt Maud**.

Rigsby: [*Approvingly*] Did you hear that laugh? Veronica sounds in sparkling mood.

[*They enter* **Rigsby**'*s room*]

9 Rigsby's room

The room is empty. **Aunt Maud** *looks around suspiciously.*

Maud: She's not here.

Rigsby: She'll be through in a minute. Why don't you sit down – dip your bread in something. No need to get suspicious.

Maud: Of course I'm suspicious. You're hiding something, I can always tell. Always were a shifty little devil. I couldn't abide you; then again, neither could your mother.

Rigsby: What do you mean? I was a lovely little chap. They used to call me Sunshine.

Maud: That's not what I called you.

Rigsby: I was always singing and laughing. Happy as the day was long. Uncle George must have remembered. I hadn't been near him for years but he left me all his money.

Maud: Yes, it must have been gratitude.

Rigsby: [*Mutters*] You're only jealous, you old bat.

Maud: [*Sharply*] What was that?

Rigsby: If I don't get the money I suppose it goes to you?

Maud: No, it goes to the dog's home.

Rigsby: The dog's home! All that money going on nourishing marrow bone jelly! What a waste! If I had that money I could travel the world, enrich my life, see strange and exotic places. [*Temptingly*] And you could share in all that, Aunt Maud.

Maud: How?

Rigsby: I could send you postcards.

Maud: Postcards!

Rigsby: And I could get your teeth fixed. You could have gold ones. You'd twinkle every time you smiled.

Maud: Are you trying to bribe a poor old age pensioner?

Rigsby: No, I've got too much respect for you – you old trout. Besides, I've got nothing to hide.

Maud: Then where is she? [*Slyly*] I heard she left you.

Rigsby: Malicious gossip, Aunt Maud. Wagging tongues – jealous of that tender shoot called happiness. Are you there, my love?

Veronica: [*Calling from another room*] I'm coming, dearest. Just freshening up.

Rigsby: She's just freshening up. I don't know if you'll recognize her. Marvellous what you can do with blue eye shadow. Then of course there was the cosmetic surgery. And she's lost weight, which has the strange effect of making her appear taller – sort of optical illusion. How is your eyesight these days?

Maud: There's nothing wrong with my eyesight.

Rigsby: [*Nervously*] Are you coming, dearest?

Veronica: [*Calling*] Coming, my love.

Rigsby: So affectionate. [**Veronica** *enters.* **Rigsby** *plants a kiss on her cheek*] Hello, my dear. You remember Aunt Maud. [*He halts. Looks again. He freezes in horror*]

Maud: It *is* Veronica.

Veronica: Of course it's Veronica. How are you Aunt Maud?

Maud: I think I'm going to have one of my turns.

Rigsby: Well, leave room for me.

Maud: I thought you'd left him?

Veronica: No, we're as happy as two turtle doves. Ain't that right, Rupert?

Rigsby: What? Yes, it's been bliss.

Maud: Well, I don't know how you've stuck it all these years. None of us thought it would last. We all thought it was a bad omen when the wedding cake collapsed.

Veronica: Ah. [*Fondly*] You don't know him. I know he doesn't look much but underneath there's a heart of gold.

Maud: Well, all I can say is you deserve some reward, Veronica, putting up with him all these years.

Veronica: You mean we get the money?

Maud: Yes, if I had my way you'd get the George Medal for gallantry as well. [*She rises*]

Veronica: You're not going?

Rigsby: [*Nervously*] Stay and have a sandwich.

Maud: No, I've seen all I want to. I never could abide him - makes my flesh creep. [*She goes out grumbling.* **Rigsby** *eyes* **Veronica** *apprehensively*]

Veronica: [*Coldly*] Who was that woman?

Rigsby: Aunt Maud?

Veronica: I mean the woman who was pretending to be me.

Rigsby: Miss Jones. She lives upstairs.

Veronica: She'll have to go. There's going to be none of that.

Rigsby: None of what?

Veronica: No hugging and squeezing, and kissing and cuddling. Not while I'm around.

Rigsby: There never was. I know why you've come back. You've heard about the money. You've come back to pick me clean. All the way from Cleethorpes. You could give flying lessons to vultures.

Veronica: [*Sweetly*] Now, Rupert - that's no way for a happily married man to talk. Remember the good times.

Rigsby: What good times? I spent most of it dodging saucepans. My ribs have only just healed. After you left I spent three years under an orthopaedic surgeon.

Veronica: Well, I bet he had more fun than I did. [*Sadly*] Didn't you miss me at all? I missed you.

Rigsby: Why? You could always have bought a punchbag.

Veronica: Didn't you miss anything about me? [*Menacingly*] What about my silvery laugh?

Rigsby: [*Nervously*] What?

Veronica: Or perhaps you don't like my laugh?

Rigsby: No, I've always found it very melodious.

Veronica: You don't think it sounds like a cross between a pneumatic drill and someone shooting crows?

Rigsby: No, the very idea. [*Pause*] Who said that?

Veronica: She did. I suppose she's refined. I suppose her laughter's like tinkling cymbals. [*She picks up handbag*] But then she's not common, is she?

Rigsby: [*Backing away*] No, Veronica – not the handbag.

Veronica: Not refined, eh? I'll show you refinement.

Rigsby: [*Frightened*] Not the handbag.

[**Veronica** *doubles* **Rigsby** *up with a blow from her handbag and then knocks him to the ground*]

10   The attic room

It is a few hours later. **Ruth** *is sticking a plaster on* **Rigsby**'s *forehead.* **Philip** *is holding the first-aid box.*

Ruth: How do you feel now, Mr Rigsby?

Rigsby: A little dizzy, Miss Jones. God. That handbag gets heavier. I think she must have had a brick in it.

Ruth: What are you going to do?

Philip: You need police protection.

Rigsby: I don't need the police. I need the Argyle and Sutherland Highlanders – and I'm not sure they'd stand firm. No, there's nothing I can do. I'm one of that neglected band of battered husbands. They don't ask questions about us in Parliament. No one cares.

Ruth: We do, Mr Rigsby. There must be something. Have you tried Marriage Guidance?

Rigsby: Yes, we tried that. We had this very nice chap – she liked him, until she found he was divorced. Then she hit him with a paperweight.

Philip: Why don't you try writing to the Problem Page? They might be able to help.

Rigsby: I did that as well but I had to be careful. I was Nervous of Leeds, Persecuted of Barnsley, Terrified of Accrington. But they never replied. It was only later I found she was Disillusioned of Doncaster. No, all you can do is turn to your friends at times like this.

Ruth: Oh, I'm sorry, Mr Rigsby – I can't stay, not after what's happened. I don't want to be Mutilated of Cheltenham.

Philip: And I can't. It's that laugh – it makes my pen jump across the page.

Rigsby: That's right, desert a sinking ship. . . . I wish I'd never heard about that money.

[**Snell** *enters*]

Snell: Ah, Mr Rigsby. I've been looking for you everywhere. I'm afraid I have some bad news. I want you to take a firm grip of yourself, old chap. [*To the others*] Stand by with the brandy.

Ruth: What's happened?

Snell: I'm afraid there's no money. Apparently George Rigsby never paid any income tax. It all goes to the Inland Revenue.

Rigsby: You mean I don't get anything?

Snell: I'm afraid not. [*Pause*] Are you all right?

Rigsby: [*Begins to laugh*] That's terrible news. Absolutely terrible. I don't know how I'm going to break it to my wife. [*More laughter*] That poor woman. Stand by with the brandy. It's a shocking disappointment, isn't it?

Veronica: [*Calling from downstairs*] Rupert!

Rigsby: [*Titters*] Coming, dear. It's tragic, really. Oh, Miss Jones – find the time of the next train to Clee-thorpes. [*He goes out*]

The end

Last of the Summer Wine

The Great Boarding-house Bathroom Caper

Roy Clarke

First shown on BBC 1 on 10 November 1976

1, 3 10, 14

Characters

Foggy
Clegg
Compo
Sid, a café proprietor
Ivy, his wife
Gordon, the minibus driver
The landlord of a pub
A traffic warden
Rose, the landlady of the Seahaven guest-house
Mabel, a waitress
Nora Batty, a neighbour of Compo

Clegg (Peter Sallis), Foggy (Brian Wilde) and Compo (Bill Owen) in the series Last of the Summer Wine *(BBC copyright)*

The Great Boarding-house Bathroom Caper

1   Inside the café

Foggy *and* **Clegg** *are sitting at a table.* **Foggy** *is looking at some postcards.*

Foggy: I'm looking forward to it. A weekend by the sea, salt air in your lungs, sun on the water.

Clegg: [*Gloomily*] Sand in your sandwiches.

Foggy: That cynical attitude doesn't fool me. You're looking forward to it just as much as I am. When I called for you this morning you were whistling.

Clegg: I'd just opened me electricity bill.

Foggy: You were happy.

Clegg: [*Whispering*] Sssh! Not so loud. Nobody admits to being happy these days. They'll think I'm weird.

Foggy: Exercise. That's what you need.

Clegg: The world's full of social reformers and there's nothing irritates your social reformer more than finding some damn fool who's happy.

Foggy: All you need is exercise. I don't keep this figure by accident, you know.

[**Sid** *enters with a broom. He is followed by* **Ivy**]

Sid: There's not a cloud in the sky. We shall be all right if this weather holds. [*He goes behind the counter*]

Ivy: Aye. We'll be able to sit here all weekend in brilliant sunshine waiting for that Gordon to turn up with his blasted minibus.

Clegg: [*To* **Foggy**] Ivy's very steady. You wouldn't catch her doing anything reckless like being happy.

[**Ivy** *overhears him. She makes a face at him but says nothing*]

Sid: He'll be here in a minute. Gordon won't let us down. The only time I've really been let down was when some fool agreed to stand as me best man.

[**Ivy** *sniffs.* **Clegg** *looks at* **Foggy** *and laughs.* **Foggy** *is in a trance*]

Clegg: Hey up, Foggy's gone again. [*He snaps his fingers in his face*] What is it, Foggy?

Foggy: [*Coming to*] Ah well – there's something missing. I was running through my mind an inventory of effects and personnel, and there's something missing.

Ivy: It's that Compo. What time does he think he's going to get here?

Foggy: I told him nine hundred hours. I gave him explicit instructions. Written down in simple terms for the average idiot. And now, of course, he has to turn out to be an above-average idiot.

Clegg: In the whole complex universe, probably my favourite class of people. Above-average idiots.

Ivy: If he can't get himself here on time, I propose we go without him.

Foggy: You can't abandon the man. You have to train him. After all he's a human being, life for the use of.

Clegg: I'd like you to know, Foggy, that you've just won the Norman Clegg Award for outstanding services to Human Lunacy.

Sid: We're not going without anybody. Why don't you get in the holiday mood? We're going to enjoy ourselves for a weekend.

Ivy: Are you sure you locked the back door?

Sid: Thirty-three times you sent me to lock that back door. I've been up since six o'clock just locking the back blasted door.

Ivy: Yes. Leaving me to do all the packing.

Sid: Packing? It's more like unpacking. [*To the others*] 'You can't tek *them*,' she keeps saying. 'I've no room for them. I haven't an inch o' space.' Then she opens her mouth.

Ivy: I heard that.

Sid: And I've been hearing that [*He indicates her mouth*] for nearly thirty blasted years. [*To her*] Have a rest, woman. You're on holiday. [*He looks out of the front door*]

Ivy: We are if the bus ever gets here.

Clegg: Foggy, how come you've got all your postcards before we even get there?

Foggy: They're cheaper here.

Clegg: That's a reckless holiday spirit.

Foggy: I've no intention of being taken for a ride.

Ivy: Just as well if you're depending on that Gordon. [*Rising*] Where the hell is he? They're all alike, his lot. Great useless heaps.

Clegg: I quite like their Arnold.

Ivy: He's just soft in the head. [*She goes out by the back door*]

Clegg: The older I get, the more I seem to like dozy people. Mind you, you get plenty of practice round here.

Foggy: Give me a razor-sharp intellect any time.

Clegg: Oh I will, the minute I find one.

Sid: Hey? What's so dozy about their Arnold? I'm the one that got married with me eyes closed, aren't I?

Clegg: I had no wish to imply, Sydney, that you weren't dozy too.

Sid: [*Not understanding*] That's all right then. [*He looks out of the front door again*]

Clegg: [*To* **Foggy**] If the weather's warm, he's the kind of person you could safely go paddling with.

Foggy: I'm looking forward to seeing Max Jaffa.

Clegg: [*A sudden thought*] Do you think he goes paddling?

Sid: [*At the front door*] Hey – he's here.

Foggy: [*Gets up and crosses to the door*] Oh dear, look at him. Why is it he never cuts the kind of figure that goes with a regimental band? [*He comes back to the table*]

Clegg: He's more your elastic band.

[**Compo** *staggers into the café carrying a suitcase tied up with string, a large cardboard box also secured with string and his wellingtons. He thumps his wellingtons down on the table*]

Sid: Here he is, then. You'd never believe he was the Duke of Devonshire, would you?

Clegg: Or the Duke of Wellington. [*He picks up the boots and takes them to the door, holding them at arm's length*]

Compo: Where are you going with them wellies?

Clegg: It's a question of survival.

Foggy: Do you really need that cardboard box?

Compo: This is me best brown hat. And I'm not having it crushed.

Foggy: It's the kind of stuff anybody normal puts out for the dustbin. Did you have to bring all this? We're not going on safari.

Compo: [*Crosses to* **Clegg**] Look at him. He stands there like a bossy giraffe.

Foggy: [*Moves towards* **Compo**, *but restrains himself*] You won't ruffle my iron self-control.

[**Foggy** *walks away, but* **Compo** *follows.* **Compo** *sits on the table and holds his legs out in front of himself*]

Clegg: Look at old Twinkle Toes.

Foggy: His trousers are half-way up his nostrils.

Compo: Will tha please kindly tek thee hands off me leg. I'm not going if it's that sort of holiday.

Sid: He looks like a ventriloquist's dummy.

Clegg: Only when you pull the string.

Compo: [*Imitating a poor ventriloquist*] Gottle of gear, gottle of gear. . . .

Foggy: I'm glad to see you've made an effort anyway.

Compo: Ta.

Foggy: At least you've tried to improve yourself.

Compo: Ta. [*He adjusts a handkerchief in his breast pocket.* **Foggy** *watches, then plucks the hanky out to find it is a used envelope. He tears it up*] What are you doing?

Foggy: Haven't you got a proper handkerchief? [**Compo** *produces one*] All right. Put it away. It might come in handy if we have to clean any bicycles.

[**Sid** *is sniffing the air suspiciously. The others take up the scent and it leads their noses towards* **Compo**. *He smirks*]

Compo: Me after-shave.

Foggy: Very subtle. I suppose if you ask for the large size you get a tanker.

Compo: It's dead masculine. It's called 'Biceps'.

Sid: Smells more like footsteps.

Compo: It's the athlete's after-shave.

Foggy: Yes. One can see they'd have to sprint a bit if they were wearing that.

Clegg: *Bi*ceps. Which obviously means half a *for*ceps, that is a pair of tweezers with only one prong. Now that could take a bit of getting used to. [*He sniffs again*] And this is going to take a bit of getting used to. Which explains why they call it 'Biceps'.

Foggy: It doesn't explain why you were late. I told you nine hundred hours.

Compo: He's off again. The Führer! Listen to him!

Foggy: This holiday is going to be run on schedule.

Compo: I couldn't help it. I had to run round at the last minute looking for somebody to leave me ferrets with.

Foggy: Couldn't you have organized a ferret sitter yesterday? Why didn't you come to someone who can organize? I would have applied a tactical brain to the problem.

Compo: I allus leave 'em next door. Wi' Nora Batty. Only when I popped round there this morning, no Nora. They've gone on holiday, an' all.

Foggy: It is a holiday weekend you know. People do go away.

Ivy: [*Re-enters*] They do if the flaming bus ever comes.

Compo: Oh, hello, Ivy. I can see you're full of the holiday spirit.

Ivy: Nice of you to come.

Compo: Give us a kiss.

[*A horn toots outside*]

Sid: Hey up, the bus is here.

[*They start gathering up their luggage.* **Ivy** *snaps open a handbag and begins to powder her face*]

Compo: Bring my case will you, Norman?

[*They troop out with their cases, except* **Ivy** *who remains standing defiantly.* **Sid** *reappears. He stands in the doorway and glares at her. She puts her compact away, snaps her bag shut and glares at* **Sid**. *She points to her case. He looks at her resignedly and picks it up. It is heavy*]

Ivy: I hope you locked that back door.

[**Sid** *groans and puts down the case. He goes out and checks the back door. He re-enters and picks up the*

case. **Sid** *and* **Ivy** *go out of the front door and lock it.*
Foggy's *postcards are still lying on the table.*
Then there is the sound of a key in the lock again.
Sid *opens up and lets* **Foggy** *back in*]

Sid: You great prongless fork. [*Mimicking* **Foggy**]
'This holiday is going to be run on schedule,' that's
what you said.

[**Foggy** *retrieves his postcards, with some em-*
barrassment. We hear tooting and jeering from
outside]

2   A main road

The minibus is parked on the hard shoulder of a dual
carriageway. It has a puncture. **Compo**, **Sid** *and* **Clegg**
are watching **Gordon** *changing the wheel.* **Foggy** *is*
trying to give helpful instructions. Eventually **Sid**,
Compo *and* **Clegg** *lead* **Foggy** *away. The back of the*
bus tilts as it is jacked up. **Ivy**, *who is still sitting inside*
it, grabs her hat and straightens it. She remains there,
her hands impatiently tapping her bag. She looks
across the road and sees a pub.

3   Inside the pub

As it is still early, the bar is fairly empty. **Compo**,
Foggy *and* **Clegg** *are seated round a table. The*
landlord *is serving* **Sid**, *who then carries pints of beer*
across to the others.

Sid: [*As he puts the beer down*] Just a quick one while
Gordon washes his hands.

Clegg: He looks very smart for a landlord, which I

always find is a sure sign that the beer's going to be untidy.

Sid: [*Sitting down*] We don't care. We're on holiday. [*The others nod in agreement and drink.* **Sid** *then reacts to what he has just said*] Well, all right. We do care a bit.

Foggy: [*Reading from a brochure*] 'Seahaven is a superior private boarding establishment with every comfort, only a short walk from the beach.' Right, who's for a swim then, every morning before breakfast? [*They ignore him*] Very well, I'll go by myself.

Compo: They don't make 'em like him any more.

Sid: They never did.

Foggy: I don't see what all the fuss is about. We could all do with the glow which comes from bodies driven to the limits.

Clegg: I think they'd like you to restrain, Foggy, what to me is one of your most endearing features. A sustained courageous determination to make a prat of yourself.

[**Foggy** *sulks*]

Compo: Now you've hurt him, Norm.

Clegg: A very handsome prat.

Compo: Come on, Foggy, you're going on holiday. I'll buy you a stick of rock, and some whelks.

Foggy: Stop going on like that. You remind me of my Auntie Bluebell. Of course, she didn't wear as much scent. Place seems fit enough for the memsahibs. I think someone ought to escort Ivy in here for a drink.

Sid: That's the second stupid idea he's had in less than a minute.

Clegg: We think it's a gift.

Compo: How long's our Gordon going to be? Does tha reckon he's got stuck in them toilets?

Sid: If he can drive a bus he should be able to steer his way through that simple operation.

Compo: I'm beginning to think he must be having trouble with his clutch. [*He unveils his wrist and consults a huge new wristwatch*] I mean, after all he must have been in there for about ten minutes.

Sid: Hey up!

Clegg: Hello, hello! That's very space age!

Foggy: Been balancing your payments again?

Compo: Our Hilda's club. Shilling a week.

Foggy: She's in for a nervous Christmas, then, isn't she?

Sid: How many dials has it got?

Compo: It's not just a watch, it's a miniature calculator.

Sid: How?

Compo: Well, I'm not too sure about that.

Sid: What's the time, then?

Compo: [*Staring intently. His face begins to screw and contort with the mental strain. The others watch him*] Uuh, uuh, uuh – if you're a balloonist it tells you how far you are under the water.

Foggy: That's useful.

Compo: Plus it's water resistant.

Foggy: Yes, I can see where that would appeal.

[**Compo** *leans forward over the table to drink his beer*]

Foggy: Where are you going?

Compo: I'm trying not to spill this beer all down my best jacket.

Foggy: You're not going to carry on like this all over the weekend, are you?

Compo: Will you stop elbowing me!

Foggy: I'm going to insist upon certain standards of behaviour.

Compo: [*Roused*] That's a typical Tory remark. I'm fed up with you going on at me. [*He is angry with* **Foggy** *and threatens him.* **Clegg** *rises and crosses to speak to the* **landlord**]

Clegg: Excuse the running battle, landlord. Only this gentleman is a stickler for etiquette and writes for the *Catering Corps Argus*, and this gentleman isn't and doesn't. Will you have one, landlord?

Landlord: [*Pointing to* **Compo** *and* **Clegg**] Not one of those two, I won't. [*Goes out to a back room*]

Clegg: [*To himself*] I meant a drink. [*He crosses back to the table*]

Compo: He's a bit chilly, isn't he?

Foggy: Is there any wonder, the way you behave? He's probably spent his life out here building up a decent clientele. Then you walk in, as if none of the Public Health Acts have ever happened.

[**Compo** *is about to argue, but* **Gordon** *enters, sits at the bar and drinks a pint that has been left there for him*]

Clegg: Hey up, Gordon.

Gordon: Nice toilets.

Clegg: Well, you stay here if you like, Gordon, but we're going on to Scarborough.

4   The promenade

The bus pulls up on a cliff top promenade in Scarborough. They all get out and walk to the railings. **Ivy** *sniffs and goes straight back into the bus.*

Sid: [*Breathing in deeply*] How about that then! Smell that air.

Compo: Fish and chips.

Clegg: And then they say he's got no poetry in him.

Foggy: It looks peaceful today, but the German navy shelled it, you know, in 1914.

Clegg: Ah yes. But I should think they'll have finished by now.

Sid: What time's high tide?

Foggy: Ask the striped gentleman in the short trousers here. He's got the world's most complicated watch.

[**Compo** *blows a raspberry at him*]

Clegg: Oh look. Your Gordon's made friends already.

[*A traffic warden is giving* **Gordon** *a parking ticket*]

5   Outside the Seahaven guest-house

The minibus drives up and stops. They start to get out. **Rose,** *the landlady, comes down the steps to greet them.* **Ivy** *shakes her hand. Then* **Foggy** *shakes her hand. He picks up his case and gives it to* **Clegg. Rose** *goes up the steps and into the guest-house, followed by*

Ivy *and* **Foggy**, *and then* **Clegg** *and* **Sid** *who are carrying the luggage.* **Compo** *follows on. They all go inside. Then* **Clegg** *comes back and calls to* **Gordon**.

Clegg: Gordon! Come on, Gordon.

6   A bedroom

There are the sounds of weary footsteps on the staircase and then the door opens to admit **Foggy**, **Clegg** *and* **Compo**, *out of breath and loaded with their luggage. They stagger to the beds and sit down.*

Compo: By! It's a pull up them stairs – five fluttering flights.

Foggy: At least the bathroom's only one floor down.

Clegg: Once the red mist starts clearing from in front of your eyes, it looks like quite a nice room.

Compo: [*Stretches out on a bed*] Well, I think I'll rest here for a while and mebbe tackle them stairs again about Wednesday. [*The luncheon gong sounds downstairs.* **Compo** *leaps up*] We're on fire!

Foggy: That's lunch.

Compo: The lunch is on fire?

Foggy: It means it's time to eat.

Compo: Well, what a damn silly way to carry on. [*He scurries off downstairs*]

Foggy: That man! [*Calling*] Walk, don't run!

Clegg: It may be a short walk to the beach but it's a perishing long way to the dining-room.

Foggy: Courage – it's downhill all the way.

7 The dining-room

Only two of the half-dozen tables are occupied. **Clegg**, **Foggy** *and* **Compo** *are at one;* **Sid**, **Ivy** *and* **Gordon** *are at the other. The meal is over and they are lingering on cigarettes and a cup of tea,*

The dreaded **Mabel**, *an ancient body in waitress's black, is clearing up.*

Foggy: I thought that was very palatable.

Clegg: Well, we're still in Yorkshire, aren't we? Not as if we'd gone abroad. Like that fool Anderson from Wortley Street.

Compo: Where did he go, then?

Clegg: Liverpool.

Compo: Oh! [*He lapses into his blank look*]

Clegg: He said the water was drinkable, though.

[*They nod sagely and hold a moment's silence out of sympathy for Anderson.* **Ivy** *sips her tea daintily.*
   Mabel *watches, unimpressed, and whips away the cup and saucer as soon as it is put down.*
   Gordon *is about to drink*]

Mabel: [*To* **Gordon**] Have you finished?

[**Gordon** *surrenders his cup hastily*]

Sid: [*To* **Mabel**] How about a refill, love?

Mabel: No thanks. I haven't time to sit supping tea all day. [*She whips* **Sid**'s *cup too and bears it away to the kitchen.* **Rose** *collides with her in the door but* **Mabel** *rescues the crockery*] Oh gracious. [**Rose** *blushes and straightens her escaping hair – wiping tea leaves on her face in the process and becoming even more confused*]

Rose: [*To the others*] I hope everything was all right.

[*General chorus of approval from the men*]

Ivy: [*In a particularly posh voice*] I was just saying how very nice everything was, Mrs Chafer. Seldom have we received such service.

[*The men react in amazement to* **Ivy**'s *performance*]

Rose: Oh, I'm glad. I wish you'd call me Rose. [*She wipes her face*] I do try. It's all right now, of course. Early season. But I get very flustered when we're full. [**Mabel** *pushes past* **Rose** *to retrieve cups, and takes them back to the kitchen*] But Mabel's a treasure.

Sid: She looks as if she's been dug up.

[**Gordon** *laughs.* **Compo** *is wrapping the bones from his plate in a paper napkin.* **Foggy** *stares at him*]

Foggy: What the devil are you up to?

Compo: I thought, seeing as we're right up top, I'd take a few scraps for the sea-gulls.

Foggy: You don't feed sea-gulls. They're like buzzards. They'll have your arm off. Or in your case your sleeve. Also they have very primitive internal arrangements. It'll go straight through like a drain-pipe and be deposited in the space that I have mentally reserved for hanging out my trunks to dry.

Clegg: [*Sees* **Mabel** *approaching and whispers*] Look out, the Gestapo's here. [*He smiles pleasantly at her. She returns him a hostile stare and starts collecting their pots. She pauses over* **Compo**'s *empty plate*]

Mabel: God! Does he eat the bones an' all?

[**Clegg** *and* **Foggy** *look innocently at her*]

8   The beach

Clegg, **Compo** *and* **Foggy** *are clambering about on some rocks.*

Compo: Why does the sea taste of salt?

Clegg: I expect they ran out of vinegar.

Foggy: It's the mineral content. The wear and tear on the rocks.

Compo: Like sliding down a fireman's pole. I've allus wanted to do that. It must be a sod though, getting back up. Especially when you're worn out after a fire. I think I've seen a winkle.

Clegg: Don't you know?

Compo: Not really. It were gone in a flash.

Clegg: [*Joins* **Compo** *and looks into a rock pool*] Never mind. They take too much training to make good pets anyway.

Foggy: What are you talking about? Dozy pair.

Compo: Winkle training. [**Foggy** *looks baffled*] They need a firm hand.

Clegg: What about affection?

Compo: Rubbish. There must have been more winkles ruined by over-pampering than any other single cause. Hey, me shoes are going green.

Foggy: From outside or in?

Compo: Outside. It's off the rocks.

Clegg: Life, you see. You start out in a morning full of hope and by tea-time your shoes are going green.

Foggy: Is it that time already? No, don't roll your sleeve up for our benefit. We're only here for a weekend.

9 An upstairs corridor

It is night-time. **Compo** *comes out of the bathroom and sits on a chair outside it.* **Ivy** *comes out of her bedroom and crosses to the bathroom. She falters as she sees* **Compo** *but then goes in the bathroom and shuts the door.*

10 The bedroom

Clegg *and* **Foggy** *are in their beds, very comfortable. They are both reading.*

Foggy: This is very pleasant. I must confess to a feeling of growing optimism about this holiday.

Clegg: [*Peers over his glasses at* **Foggy**] It wasn't you on the bridge that night, steering the Titanic, was it?

Foggy: I refuse to be discouraged. [*He points to* **Compo**'s *empty bed*] Things are looking up. He's been exposed to my civilizing influence and it's beginning to pay.

Clegg: He's been exposed in all sorts of places in his day. I'm looking forward to seeing his best brown hat.

Foggy: Have you had a peep at his socks lately?

Clegg: [*Snaps his fingers*] I knew there was something I meant to do. Now, come on, Foggy. We can't cram everything into the first day.

Foggy: You might be pleasantly surprised. I was. I came here in the full expectation that the only way to make the nights tolerable would be to banish his socks to the fire escape. And with that purpose in mind I approached them gingerly and turned them over with the sharp end of my combination ruler and spirit level.

Clegg: You've got nerve, Foggy. I'll say that for you.

Foggy: Only to find that they are brand new, relatively harmless and, what's more, his feet are clean.

Clegg: Could he have sneaked off and had a paddle?

Foggy: No. I think he's been washing 'em.

Clegg: The whole world's upside down.

Foggy: And what's more – this is the third time this evening he's been down with his towel to the bathroom.

11   The corridor

We see **Compo** *waiting patiently – even happily – outside the occupied bathroom. He is wearing a dressing-gown stencilled 'Property of Huddersfield public baths', his towel round his neck.*

Ivy *comes out of the bathroom. She pulls her dressing-gown more securely over her nightdress as she sees him.*

Ivy: Are you planning on being here every time I use the bathroom?

Compo: Well I don't know about every time, Ivy love. [*He ogles her admiringly*] I don't get up too early of a morning. But I'll catch thee every bed-time, wi' a bit a luck. [*He pats her bottom as she flees into her own room. He sighs contentedly when she's gone and he hears her door lock*]

Gordon: [*Appearing gloomily in his pyjamas*] Early to bed and early to rise, Makes a man healthy and

wealthy and bored. [*He pauses at the bathroom door*]
Are you waiting to go in, Uncle Bill?

Compo: Tha must be joking. It's much more fun out here.

12   The bedroom

Foggy *and* **Clegg** *are still reading in bed as* **Compo** *comes in, still in his dressing-gown and with his towel round his neck. He is singing cheerfully.*

Compo: 'Hold my hand. I'm a stranger in Paradise.' I think I'm going to like it here. There's more to see here than there is at home.

Clegg: Oh, he looks just like Henry Cooper.

Foggy: But he sings like him too.

Compo: There's another couple staying downstairs. Next to Gordon's room. I could hear 'em arguing.

Foggy: I hope you haven't been earwigging.

Compo: No. I were just passing.

Clegg: You've been 'just passing' quite a lot, haven't you? How many times have you been to the bathroom?

Compo: I'm just getting the feel o' the place. [*He listens at the open door*] I'll tell thee what's just occurred to me. Why don't I go and wash me feet? [*He slips out eagerly and they stare at each other in puzzlement*]

13   The corridor

Compo *is waiting outside the bathroom door again. We can hear a female singing and gargling. The door* *finally opens and* **Nora Batty** *comes out. They gape at each other.*

Compo: Nora Batty, my own true love!

Nora: Oh God! What are you doing here?

Compo: Oh, I love thee, Nora.

Nora: Don't you come near me.

Compo: Hast tha run away and left him – hast tha left him in the lurch?

Nora: No, I've left 'im in the bedroom.

Compo: Eh, my cup is running over. And it looks as if thine might be spilling a bit. [*He looks at her chest. Then chases her shrieking into her room*] You'll be all right tonight, Wally.

4   The bedroom

The room is in darkness, with all apparently asleep. Then **Foggy** *hears something and sits up abruptly and turns the light on.*

Clegg: What's wrong?

Foggy: Ssshhh.

Clegg: Eh?

Foggy: Shush.

Clegg: Shush? A moment ago I was full of shush. It's you that's started me off.

Foggy: I keep hearing something.

Clegg: Yes. It's some dozy herbert saying shush.

Foggy: Listen!

Clegg: Nothing.

Foggy: You forget I've got a trained soldier's reflex. One crack of a twig and I'm reaching for me bayonet.

Clegg: Well, who the hell's going to be cracking twigs up here?

Foggy: It's haunted. This place is haunted. Else they've got mice.

Clegg: You mean terrifying, chain-rattling, risen-from-the-grave mice? With fangs?

Foggy: If you don't believe me, listen. They're in the wardrobe.

Compo: [*Sitting up*] It's a seagull.

Foggy: In the wardrobe?

Compo: No. Moving about. It just sounds like it's in the wardrobe.

Foggy: I see. It does impressions. Throws its voice into this wardrobe.

Compo: Go to sleep.

Foggy: I'm going to investigate.

Compo: [*Leaps out of bed*] Stay theeself still. I'll do it. [*He opens the wardrobe door and closes it again immediately*] I telled thee there's nowt there.

Foggy: You don't call that investigating.

Compo: [*Bars* **Foggy***'s way*] Listen, why don't we go and have a walk on the sea front while it's not crowded. I bet we could get a seat now.

Foggy: What *is* he trying to hide?

Clegg: Very little from this angle. Would you mind adjusting his dress?

Foggy: [*Emerges from the wardrobe bearing* **Compo***'s box*] They've got inside your box.

Compo: Well leave 'em. I don't mind 'em being in there. I can't enjoy my holiday if we have to throw some poor little creature out in the cold.

Foggy: You can't have mice swarming about in your personal belongings! [*He opens the box.* **Compo** *snatches it back*] His ferrets! He's brought his blasted ferrets.

Clegg: That Henry Cooper - never goes anywhere without his ferrets.

Foggy: Get 'em out on that fire escape! You're not keeping 'em in here. And now we're going to be all weekend trying to conceal his chattering ferrets!!!

The end

Going Straight

Going to be All Right

Dick Clement and Ian la Frenais

First shown on BBC 1 on 3 March 1978

Characters

Fletcher, an ex-prisoner
Lennie Godber, his former cell-mate
Ingrid, Fletcher's daughter (aged 26)
Mrs Chapman, Fletcher's probation officer
Raymond, Fletcher's teenage son
Men in the probation office
Man in the country

Fletcher (Ronnie Barker), the incorrigible criminal, being released on parole in the series Going Straight *(BBC copyright)*

Going to be All Right

---

1 Probation office

There are two men sitting waiting. **Fletcher** *enters.*

Fletcher: [*Sitting down*] Aye aye. [*Pause. He looks around*] Gawd, look at this place! Hasn't had a coat of paint since I was here last. Oppressive, in'it? I mean, you feels guilty just walking in the door. Liable to admit to all sorts of things you never done. Know what I mean? [*The other two look blank.* **Fletcher** *leans forward to inspect the magazines*] Same old magazines, I see. *The British Felon, The Safe-cracker's Weekly.* [*No reaction*] Just a joke. Well you've got to, ain't you – ain't you? [*He points to an inner office*] Anyone in there, is there? [*One man nods*] And there's you two before me. Still, I can bide me time. Used to that, aren't we? Ironical, though, really. One of the main things they tells you on parole is, don't mix with bad company. Then you sit out here for an hour with a couple of villains like you. This is the one place you're guaranteed bad company, ain't it?

First man: What makes you think we're bad company?

Fletcher: What? You're here in't you, for starters.

Besides which, I know the criminal mentality. Too many years spent in their company. Certain signs are dead give-aways. I mean, you two – hard lads, ain't you? Taciturn. GBH. Assault with a deadly weapon. It's written all over you.

[*The men react indignantly*]

Second man: We're here to give a quote on the decorating.

Fletcher: Oh, well – assault with a deadly distemper brush.

[*The inner door opens and a burly man leaves followed by* **Mrs Chapman**]

Mrs Chapman: Mr Fletcher?

Fletcher: Yes.

Mrs Chapman: [*To men*] I won't keep you a minute.

[*He follows her into her office*]

2 Mrs Chapman's office

Mrs Chapman: Sit down, please.

Fletcher: [*Shuts the door*] Thank you.

Mrs Chapman: [*Introducing herself*] Mrs Chapman – Mrs Shirley Chapman. [*They shake hands.* **Fletcher** *produces a piece of paper*]

Fletcher: You'll want this, will you? My dog licence.

Mrs Chapman: [*Correcting him*] Your parole licence.

Fletcher: Same thing, in'it? Got me on a leash, ain't you?

Mrs Chapman: There are certain conditions of

parole you're expected to comply with. If you don't like it you can go back in and finish your porridge.

Fletcher: No, no. I'll go along with whatever you say.

Mrs Chapman: [*Sitting at her desk*] In your case it's not too difficult. You report weekly to me, you stay out of the company that you previously mixed with, and as soon as possible you start the gainful employment which you guaranteed as part of your application for parole.

Fletcher: Ah, the job, yes. We may have a bit of a problem there.

Mrs Chapman: Problem?

Fletcher: Well, you see, Isobel, my wife, she fixed me up with that job.

Mrs Chapman: The cardboard box factory.

Fletcher: On the North Circular, yeah. See, Isobel was very friendly with the owner – bloke called Jessop, Reg Jessop. It was him what guaranteed the gainful employment.

Mrs Chapman: I know, I have his letter on the file.

Fletcher: Well, the trouble is, in the intervening period since the letter, the friendship between her and Reg Jessop has blossomed.

Mrs Chapman: Blossomed?

Fletcher: Well yeah . . . or put it another way, they now live together.

Mrs Chapman: Live together?

Fletcher: Yeah, together, both at once. Co-habit, I think the phrase is. So there's no way I'm going to work for a bloke called Reg who's shacked up with my old lady.

Mrs Chapman: But this is terrible. I had to submit your home circumstances report to endorse your application for parole.

Fletcher: Yeah.

Mrs Chapman: In which I stated that those home circumstances were stable.

Fletcher: Oh, they're stable all right – but the horse has bolted. Or in this case, the old mare. Still, give Isobel her due – she didn't let on, did she? She didn't mess up my parole.

Mrs Chapman: But the two most important factors in obtaining a parole are (a) marriage and (b) employment. Here you are out and I find you have neither.

Fletcher: If you put it that way I suppose that's true, yeah.

Mrs Chapman: This puts me in a most embarrassing position.

Fletcher: Don't do me much good either – lot worse for me, isn't it, girl? My life, in ruins around me.

Mrs Chapman: You don't seem particularly devastated. But then I suppose you knew well in advance.

Fletcher: Me? No. A bombshell. Take me a while to get over it. If I ever do. What I really need is a period of readjustment – by the seaside, something like that.

Mrs Chapman: Mr Fletcher, we have a practical problem here. Your wife supported your home and family while you were in prison.

Fletcher: Well, yes, she had a good job.

Mrs Chapman: Manageress of a dry cleaner's, wasn't it?

Fletcher: Yeah – we were never short of coat hangers. That was before he came along, Rollicking Reg Jessop, the Cardboard King.

Mrs Chapman: Then I imagine that since him your wife's income will not be coming into the house?

Fletcher: No, it won't, no. She don't work no longer. Lives in the lap of luxury up near Chingford.

Mrs Chapman: You still have a family to support though. And the mortgage payments to make.

Fletcher: Oh, that's all right. My two daughters work – Ingrid and Marion.

Mrs Chapman: So you're quite content, are you, to be supported by the female members of your family?

Fletcher: Well, the trouble is my son Raymond's still at school. But don't worry, it's his last term. Then he can chip in with the rest of them.

Mrs Chapman: I've had a thought!

Fletcher: Oh yes?

Mrs Chapman: Is this too outrageous?

Fletcher: Dunno.

Mrs Chapman: *You* work. You assume some of the responsibility that others in your family have borne all the years you've been inside.

Fletcher: I intend to work! I just ain't going to work for my wife's cardboard lover.

Mrs Chapman: Mr Fletcher, I don't want to give you a bad time. My job's to help you. Why do you think I'm here – for the money?

Fletcher: Oh, you must earn a decent screw, don't you?

Mrs Chapman: Not when you support a husband and two kids.

Fletcher: Oh, he sits at home, does he? Quite content to live off a woman?

Mrs Chapman: He sits at home because he can't find a job.

Fletcher: Can't you find him one?

Mrs Chapman: Not in his field.

Fletcher: Not in his field. Oh, I see – he's a farmer.

Mrs Chapman: He's an aero-space engineer. Perhaps that tells you how tough it is out there.

Fletcher: Oh well, fat chance I've got of getting off the ground.

Mrs Chapman: We'll find you something. And you'll take what you can get.

Fletcher: Righty-oh, then. I'll check in next week and see what's turned up.

Mrs Chapman: Unless I get in touch with you before then.

Fletcher: No mad rush.

Mrs Chapman: Meanwhile, sign on. How are you fixed for cash?

Fletcher: Well, I did have all the money I'd earned while I was inside, but I blew that as soon as I got off the train.

Mrs Chapman: In a betting shop? Or a pub?

Fletcher: Neither. As a matter of fact, I got two bars of fruit and nut out of a slot machine.

3 Fletcher's house

It is evening. In the living-room, **Ingrid** *is curling her hair with electric tongs when* **Fletcher** *enters.*

Ingrid: Hello, dad.

Fletcher: Hello, gel.

Ingrid: What sort of a day have you had?

Fletcher: Any tea in the teapot?

Ingrid: No, but you can put the kettle on.

Fletcher: Oh no, it doesn't matter.

Ingrid: I said what sort of a day have you had?

Fletcher: What time do we eat around here?

Ingrid: Well, I'm going out. And Raymond's eaten. But he can always pop down the road and fetch you something from the new take-away kebab house.

Fletcher: What happened to all those nice old English traditional take-away Chinese restaurants we had? I thought we'd have a nice hot dinner in – just the family.

Ingrid: Well, we've all made plans. What sort of day d'you have then?

Fletcher: Not bad. Had a swift half at the White Hart. Pint and a pie at the Anchor. Signed on the Labour, of course. Had a swift half at the Magpie. Then I dropped by the Old Ship for a swift half en route to the Rainbow Club.

Ingrid: Why did you go down the Rainbow?

Fletcher: Nowhere else to get a drink Tuesday afternoon.

Ingrid: You're not supposed to mix with bad company.

Fletcher: I didn't – I sat on me own.

Ingrid: What, down there? You'd see all your old crowd.

Fletcher: No, no – the old crowd's gone, they're all inside now.

Ingrid: See your probation officer?

Fletcher: Course I did. Right little tartar, she is.

Ingrid: Yes. I thought, when I met her, when she was compiling her report on your domestic circs, she's no fool, I thought. Don't suppose she was taken in for one minute by your broken-hearted act. 'How can I do a job of work with my life shattered?'

Fletcher: My life is shattered. I told her, bombshell.

Ingrid: Oh, leave it out, dad. You knew the situation months back.

Fletcher: Yeah, but it's only hit me now. Getting home to a house without her. No kettle on. No dinner in the oven. [*He gets up and switches the television on. It is* Playschool] Oh! [*He switches it off*]

Ingrid: That's all mum was to you. A housekeeper.

Fletcher: How could she abandon you kids?

Ingrid: Abandon? Abandon?

Fletcher: Well, scarper off with another bloke.

Ingrid: Dad, I'm twenty-six. And it's been two years since Marion lived in this house on a regular basis.

Fletcher: What about Raymond? He's a schoolboy.

Ingrid: Only just. And let me tell you, mum did not scarper until Raymond had sat his last A-level.

Raymond: [*Enters*] Seen my Led Zeppelin tape?

Ingrid: Don't ask me, Raymond. You leave things all over the place.

Raymond: What time is it?

Ingrid: Ten to.

Raymond: Seen my bicycle pump?

Ingrid: It's in the lav – though gawd knows why.

Fletcher: [*Listening to this exchange with fascination*] Hello, son, how's it going, then?

Raymond: I can't shake off this catarrh. Ingrid, you seen my extendable steel tape measure?

Ingrid: Oh, Raymond, do you really need it this minute?

Raymond: No. What time is it?

Ingrid: Ten to!

Raymond: [*Without urgency*] I'm late then. [*He wanders out listlessly*]

Fletcher: [*Watching his only son leave with bewildered horror*] What did he take his A-level in then – lethargy?

Ingrid: He's quite bright. Academically.

Fletcher: He seems to lack something. Charm, for starters.

Ingrid: Mmm. That's what his school report said. Bright but surly.

Fletcher: Needs a new battery, if you ask me. You know, since I got back he's hardly exchanged two words with me.

Ingrid: Being the youngest, he's seen the least of you over the years, dad.

Fletcher: So?

Ingrid: Maybe he's not sure who you are and is afraid to ask.

Fletcher: He's withdrawn into a shell because his mum's left him.

Ingrid: Dad, mum owes this family nothing. The reason this family's intact, the reason we've got what we have, is all down to mum. We've all grown up now, and mum's got the chance to snatch a few years' comfort and luxury.

Fletcher: So it's comfort and luxury she wants, is it?

Ingrid: Don't we all?

Fletcher: Well, I'm here to provide that.

Ingrid: Good, you can start with the garden. No one's touched it for a year. It's like that Matto Grosso out there.

Fletcher: The what?

Ingrid: Matto Grosso. It's a deep impenetrable jungle. *The World About Us*, BBC 2.

Fletcher: Look, I ain't come home to reclaim a jungle. I'm here to provide all the things this family apparently lacks.

Ingrid: On what you draw from the Labour?

Fletcher: Now, you just listen to me, Miss Nifty-Knickers.

Ingrid: I've got to iron my dress.

Fletcher: Sit down there [*Pushing her down into a chair*] and listen to me. [*She starts to get up*] Sit down. My motto has always been that it pays to plan ahead. To put something aside for that rainy day.

Ingrid: Oh blast, I've broken a nail.

Fletcher: Ingrid! Listen to me.

Ingrid: Sorry, dad.

Fletcher: I'm trying to tell you that, way back, unbeknownst to you, I put aside a little nest egg. For the future – which is now.

Ingrid: Did you?

Fletcher: Yes – we're going to be all right, girl. All of us.

Ingrid: D'you mean like Post Office Savings, building society, something like that?

Fletcher: No, not exactly. My little nest egg is – well, it's buried in a turnip field in Essex.

Ingrid: Wouldn't it have been safer in a bank?

Fletcher: No. It was a bank it came out of.

Ingrid: A bank! Stolen money?

Fletcher: Sssh! Raymond'll hear.

Ingrid: So that's why you've had no anxieties about getting a job. This is the 'going straight' we keep hearing about. [*She goes into the kitchen*]

Fletcher: [*Following her*] I am going straight. That cash is for us. A few thousand quid.... [*Quieter*] A few thousand quid. It's a cushion against the harsh realities which I don't want to impose on my family.

Ingrid: This family don't need it, dad. This family's got by without it.

Fletcher: I want to give you things. All of you. And maybe your mum'll come back if she knows I've got more than promises to offer her.

Ingrid: No, she won't. All she ever wanted, all any of us ever wanted, was an honest wage in this house; not a dishonest cushion. [*She goes back into the living-room*]

Fletcher: [*Following her*] I intend to make an honest wage. But it's not that easy you know, with a record.

Ingrid: No, it's not easy. But I know someone who done it.

Fletcher: Who?

Ingrid: Leonard.

Fletcher: Leonard?

Ingrid: Lennie, then.

Fletcher: Young Godber! You're seeing him, are you?

Ingrid: We keep in touch. And he's doing all right. Even though he's got a job he don't like much, he's prepared to take the rough with the smooth.

Fletcher: What is he – a French polisher?

Ingrid: No dad, he's got a driving job. Heavy goods.

Fletcher: You can do better than him, you know.

Ingrid: I'm the judge of that.

Fletcher: When do you see him then?

Ingrid: When I can.

Fletcher: Well, who are you titivating yourself for tonight then? Filing your nails and curling your hair and ironing your dress?

Ingrid: Leonard.

Fletcher: Oh, he's in London, is he?

Ingrid: Yeah. He's upstairs having a shave.

[**Fletcher** *reacts in amazement*]

4   A pub

It is later the same evening. **Fletcher** *is sitting moodily at a table nursing a pint.* **Lennie** *crosses from the bar with two drinks.*

Lennie: Here you are, Fletch. . . . [*He sits down*] Good to see you – welcome home. [*Pause*] Took me a while to find you.

Fletcher: I told Ingrid I was going to the local.

Lennie: But you've got about twenty locals. Cheers. [*He drinks*]

Fletcher: Shaved, have you?

Lennie: Yeah.

Fletcher: D'you use one of my blades?

Lennie: Oh, come on, Fletch. We're not inside now....

Fletcher: You obviously did then.

Lennie: As a matter of fact I used one of Raymond's.

Fletcher: Oh, he shaves, does he?

Lennie: Only just.

Fletcher: You'd know, of course. Being a resident in my house.

Lennie: Only twice a week. I still live in Brum.

Fletcher: Twice a week, is it? I bet you pockets your bed and board allowance.

Lennie: I can do with every penny, Fletch. [*Pause*] Ingrid's upset.

Fletcher: Why?

Lennie: You know.

Fletcher: Do I?

Lennie: Yeah.

Fletcher: Why?

Lennie: You know!

Fletcher: Look, you tell me she's upset. I'm asking why?

Lennie: Because of your nest egg.

Fletcher: She told you about that!

Lennie: I knew about it, anyway.

Fletcher: How?

Lennie: You told me – one night inside.

Fletcher: I can't have. I never talk about it.

Lennie: You had one too many.

Fletcher: One too many what?

Lennie: Prune vodkas.

Fletcher: I don't remember.

Lennie: Few people do after your prune vodkas. [*Laughs*] Thought you were going straight.

Fletcher: I am going straight. Straight to that turnip field in Essex.

Lennie: Oh, come on, Fletch!

Fletcher: Listen! That nest egg was a legacy from way back. It's just to enable me to get on the right financial footing to start with. I've paid my dues.

Lennie: Not for this job, you ain't.

Fletcher: Academic.

Lennie: All right, so you dig it up. And you come down here and it's doubles, new washing machine, down payment on a new Cortina.

Fletcher: I wasn't born yesterday, sonny Jim. I'm not going to put it around like Jack the lad.

Lennie: Not much use to you then, is it?

Fletcher: Shove off, will you?

Lennie: I'm in no hurry.

Fletcher: You will be if I kick you through that door.

Lennie: 'Man who strikes the first blow admits that his arguments have run out.' Chinese proverb.

Fletcher: 'Man who gets fist in mouth, cannot no longer give lip.' Muswell Hill proverb.

Lennie: How can you say you're going straight, then start life off on the proceeds of illicit gain? Oh, come on Fletch, forget about the money – it's not worth it. Your family don't want that.

Fletcher: It would appear my family don't want me at all. My son Raymond ignores me. All he's interested in is his extendable tape measure and his bicycle pump. My daughter Marion hasn't even been to see me yet. Called up to say hello and reversed the charges. As for my daughter Ingrid, she's taken up with some poncey long-distance lorry driver, name of Leonard.

Lennie: [*Gently*] They still love you, Fletch.

Fletcher: Yeah, like my old lady does. Her what lives in the lap of luxury with Jessop the box-maker. She knew which side her cardboard's buttered.

Lennie: They all care. See, I know because . . . well, I know them all better than what you do now.

Fletcher: Oh, you think so, do you?

Lennie: I know they love you.

Fletcher: It's their respect I would like, Lennie, their respect. Funny thing is, I had respect in the nick. I knew where I stood there, and the people round me. Precious little respect out here. Stuck at the end of a dole queue or working Paddington parcels. Money's respect, Len. Money's independence. You can face the rest of the world and say, 'I upped my income, so up yours.'

Lennie: Well, well, I always thought you had more bottle than that.

Fletcher: More bottle than what?

Lennie: Than what you've apparently got. Look, Fletch, I'm beholden to you and your family because of what you taught me inside, and for what Ingrid's done for me since I came out. So one way or another I'm not going to let you ruin your life or theirs. Look, forget the money – it's not worth it.

Fletcher: What?

Lennie: Try it, will you – try it.

Fletcher: All right, all right.

Lennie: Promise.

Fletcher: Look, I've said all right. If I say I'll try, I'll try.

5   A street

Fletcher *comes out of an ironmonger's with a spade. He walks along the street, carrying the spade. He meets* **Ingrid** *unexpectedly.*

Ingrid: Hello, dad.

Fletcher: What?

Ingrid: What are you doing with that spade?

Fletcher: What spade?

Ingrid: The one on your shoulder.

Fletcher: Oh, that spade.

Ingrid: Yes, that gleaming new spade. Which matches the gleam in your eye.

Fletcher: I just bought it. What's wrong with that?

Ingrid: Spades dig things up.

Fletcher: I know, I'm ... going to ... start work on the garden, in't I?

Ingrid: Oh good.

[**Ingrid** *leaves him. He makes a face at her back*]

6 Fletcher's garden

Fletcher *is digging.* **Ingrid** *looks out of a window.* **Fletcher** *turns and she waves to him.*

Fletcher: [*Shouting*] What is this, blinking surveillance?

[**Ingrid** *nods a 'yes'.* **Fletcher** *turns back to his digging*]

7 Fletcher's living-room

Lennie *is looking out of the window when* **Ingrid** comes in with a cup of tea for him.

Ingrid: Here y'are, love.

Lennie: He's done a heck of a job on the garden.

Ingrid: Yes, he never stopped. [*Laughs*]

Lennie: Where is he now?

Ingrid: Down the chemist's getting something for his blisters.

Lennie: Here, he might. . . .

Ingrid: It's all right. Raymond's tailing him.

Lennie: How long can we keep this up - watching him every minute? Following him about.

Ingrid: What else can we do? We got to save him from himself. D'you have to go back tonight?

Lennie: I should do.

Ingrid: Oh.

Lennie: Unless I left first thing.

Ingrid: I think you should, don't you? Here, you don't

think he really bought that spade to do the garden, do you?

Lennie: No.

Ingrid: No, I don't neither.

Fletcher: [*Entering*] Here, here, that's enough of that.

Lennie: 'Lo, Fletch.

Fletcher: Just unhand him, will you?

Ingrid: Want a cup of tea, dad?

Fletcher: Yes, ta. [*He takes* **Lennie**'s *cup which* **Lennie** *has just picked up*]

Ingrid: I'll get you another one. [*She goes to the kitchen*]

Fletcher: No, one's enough. Is that your lorry parked outside?

Lennie: Yeah.

Fletcher: Best be on your way then, hadn't you? You've got twelve punctures.

Lennie: I don't have to be back till eight in the morning.

Fletcher: Meaning?

Ingrid: [*From the kitchen*] He's staying the night.

Fletcher: [*Pointing to the sofa*] On that you are, then.

Lennie: Where else?

Raymond: [*Enters*] Seen my earphones?

Lennie: Sorry, Raymond, I haven't.

Raymond: What time is it?

Lennie: Ten past.

Raymond: Oh. I've missed it then.

Fletcher: Then you shouldn't have accompanied me to the shops, should you?

Raymond: Did you notice?

Fletcher: Did I notice!

Raymond: I thought I'd took advantage of the natural cover.

Fletcher: Oh, yeah – standing behind that lamp-post, your ears were sticking out either side. I know what you're up to, all of you. Pathetic.

Ingrid: [*Coming back with a cup of tea*] Not up to anything, dad.

Lennie: What you done today, Fletch?

Fletcher: Oh, I had a very full and exciting day. Did the garden, had a fishcake for me lunch, and went down the shoe repairer's. It's all there in his report – the Bionic Man.

Ingrid: Why did you go to the shoe shop? Your shoes are all right.

Fletcher: When I come out of nick they gave me this box with my personal effects. In which there was a shoe repairer's ticket for one pair of brown brogues, soled and heeled.

Ingrid: But that was nigh on three years ago. Did you think they'd still be there?

Fletcher: Well, no harm, was there? I was passing.

Ingrid: What did they say?

Fletcher: Said they'll be ready Thursday.

8 Fletcher's living room

It is much later that night. On the settee there is the shape of a sleeping body.

Fletcher *comes in with his spade. He looks at the settee, crosses to* **Lennie***'s jacket and looks in a pocket. He gets a bunch of keys, bumps into something and listens for a reaction. There is silence. He crosses back to the settee and listens again. He pulls back the blanket and we see cushions arranged in the shape of a body.* **Fletcher** *reacts then goes out.*

9   The street

Fletcher *comes out of the house and shuts the front door quietly. He kicks over a milk bottle by mistake and walks quickly down the drive. He gets into* **Lennie***'s lorry and switches on the ignition. The lights go on in a bedroom.* **Fletcher** *starts to drive off.* **Ingrid** *comes to the window. She looks out and reacts in horror as the lorry moves off. More lights come on in the house.* **Ingrid** *comes running out.*

Ingrid: [*Shouting*] Dad. . . . [*The lorry drives off down the road*] Dad. . . .

10   Fletcher's living room

Lennie *comes in from upstairs pulling on a tee-shirt.* **Ingrid** *comes back in through the front door.*

Ingrid: He's gone.

Lennie: He's taken my lorry.

Ingrid: What am I going to do, Lenny?

Lennie: What am *I* going to do? I'm supposed to be back at the depot in Brum by eight o'clock.

Ingrid: You shouldn't have left your jacket down here

with those keys.

Lennie: Oh, I knew it would be my fault.

Ingrid: I tell you what. Ring the police and report your lorry stolen. Chances are they'll apprehend him before he reaches Essex.

Lennie: Oh, that's a lot of help for a bloke what's on parole, isn't it?

Raymond: [*Enters*] What time is it?

Ingrid: Five o'clock, go to bed.

Raymond: What's going on?

Ingrid: It's your dad. He's given us the slip.

Lennie: He's took my lorry.

Raymond: Oh, so he's gone to dig it up, has he?

Ingrid: It's everything we didn't want to happen. It's criminal. It's immoral. I'll never speak to him again, I want nothing more to do with him.

Raymond: Still, he might get away with it.

Ingrid: Even if he does.

Raymond: No, but if he does. . . .

Ingrid: What?

Raymond: I want a motorbike.

11 The countryside

Fletcher *gets out of the lorry in the countryside. He takes his spade from the cab, looks at a map and moves off. He walks some distance, stops, looks at his map again and then moves on.*

He climbs the brow of a hill and is faced by a building site. He reacts and then moves on.

He walks past several houses, counting. He stops at one, and knocks at the door. A man opens it.

Man: What do you want?

Fletcher: What?

Man: I said, what do you want? Who are you?

Fletcher: Er - I was just - er, any gardening required? Want your grass cutting? [*He looks around the garden*] Crazy-paving want straightening up or anything?

Man: Well, you could make a start on digging the hole for the lily pond if you like.

Fletcher: Oh, nice. Lily pond, is it?

Man: Well, if you'd like to follow me I'll show you where we want to put it.

Fletcher: You wouldn't rather have it just here, would you?

12 Fletcher's living room

A disconsolate **Fletcher** *sits in his armchair, both hands bandaged.* **Lennie** *and* **Raymond** *sit watching him.* **Ingrid** *gives him a cup of tea.*

Ingrid: Well, all I can say is, thank heavens. We wasn't going to speak to you again. And you got Len into trouble.

Fletcher: Didn't expect to be away so long, did I? Won't get the sack or anything, will you, son?

Lennie: I rang them up. Said I'd broken down. They said get it fixed and bring a load up tomorrow.

Fletcher: It's right there. Can't be more than a few feet under. Here, I know, we could sell this house and buy theirs.

Ingrid: What and have you digging up the floors of

Going Straight   171

each room one by one?

Fletcher: Save hoovering, wouldn't it?

Lennie: Yeah – you could grow a lawn instead of carpet. You wouldn't hoover it, you could mow it.

Fletcher: All right, all right.

Lennie: Probably been found by now anyway.

Fletcher: How?

Lennie: When they built that estate. Probably a couple of Irish drain-layers living it up in Palma by now.

[**Fletcher** *glares at him*]

Ingrid: Well, if they are it's probably ruined their lives. Too much too soon. Anyway, nuff said, dad. One bit of good news today.

Fletcher: What?

Ingrid: Your probation officer rang.

Fletcher: Oh, yeah?

Ingrid: Got you a job already. Fancy that.

Fletcher: What kind of job?

Ingrid: With the Council – local government.

Fletcher: [*Insistently*] What kind of job?

Ingrid: Down Wilmslow Road.

Fletcher: What are the Council doing down Wilmslow Road?

[*Pause.* **Ingrid** *looks to* **Lennie** *indicating to tell him*]

Lennie: Digging it up.

[**Fletcher** *reacts*]

The end

Follow-up Activities

Discussion

1   Which situation comedies do you like best? Why? Which ones do you find boring or unfunny? Why?

2   Why do you think the shows represented in this book proved popular on television?

3   Do you think some series are intended for particular groups of people? For example, do you think some series are intended especially for older people?

4   Sometimes people describe humour as being either 'coarse' or 'sophisticated'. What do they mean by such labels? What other labels could be applied to each of the scripts in this collection?

5   How do class divisions and class consciousness figure in situation comedy?

6   These scripts include Liverpudlian, Yorkshire and Cockney characters. Are regional characters funny? Are jokes about particular groups of people wrong in any way?

7   Are any subjects or situations unsuitable for a comedy series? Should comedy be censored? What makes a 'good' joke?

8   Is laughter cruel? How can it be uplifting or liberating? How can it be used as a weapon?

9   Why do you think many producers of situation

comedy shows like to record them in front of studio audiences?

10 Do you like watching new comedy series or do you prefer ones you know?

Drama

1 Many a comedy sketch has begun as an improvisation. In pairs, try improvising conversations from these starting lines:

'I see you're keeping an elephant in your back garden!'

'So you've just won the pools?'

'So your new lodger plays the bagpipes?'

'Cod and chips, fifty-three times, please.'

'Great-aunt Jane is coming to stay tomorrow.'

'We're going for a holiday in Manchester?'

Note that each improvisation will be more successful if the second speaker 'accepts' the opening line (that is, if he or she says 'yes' to the opening line).

2 Tape-record and then transcribe similar comic dialogues. Try editing and revising them to produce 'tighter' and funnier scripts, omitting anything that is unnecessary or unfunny.

3 In groups of four or five, try developing (through discussion and improvisation) your own situation comedy. Decide first on the location. It must obviously be a place where a small group of characters meet regularly and where a number of different events or episodes can occur. It might be a domestic setting, such as a kitchen or dining room or it might be a caravan or camp-site, the back room of a shop, the staffroom of a primary school, etc. (Note that it should not be a place where many 'outsiders' appear.) Next, decide on the regular characters and then try out a number of story-lines until you find

ones that are genuinely funny. Rehearse and revise your show until you are ready to show it to an audience.

4 Adapt one of the scripts in this book so that it can be tape-recorded. (See the section on 'Notes on Presentation', earlier in this book.)

Writing

1 Write about a time when you thought something serious had happened to someone close to you, but it later turned out that he or she was all right.

2 Describe a time you have found some of your old toys or other belongings. What memories did they bring back?

3 Tell the story of a time you have stayed with people you did not know all that well.

4 Describe a hotel or boarding-house you have stayed in.

5 Write about visiting a place you used to know well and finding it has altered while you were away.

6 Write a short story called either 'The Interview', 'The Day Trip' or 'The Home-coming'.

7 Try writing a comic short story or playlet about something that once happened to you (possibly something you have been reminded of while reading one of the scripts in this book), which you did not find amusing at the time but which you can laugh about now.

8 Try rewriting one of the scripts in this book as a short story.

9 Write another episode for one of the series represented in this collection or for a situation comedy series you know well. (Do not introduce more than one new character.)

10 Try planning your own new situation comedy

series. Decide on its setting, the main characters
and think up a number of story-lines for different
episodes. Then try writing one or two scenes of a
particular episode.

NB Most situation comedy series are written by
established professional writers, though ideas may be
considered by the script editor of the BBC Light Entertainment Group at the BBC Television Centre, London
W12 8QT, or by heads of light entertainment at those
independent companies involved in making comedy
series. The beginner may have some success by trying
to write for radio. Situation comedy scripts (which will
normally be of thirty minutes' length) should be sent to
the Script Editor, Light Entertainment (Radio), BBC,
Broadcasting House, London W1A 1AA. Decisions will
be made only on complete scripts *which must be clearly
typed*. All material must be submitted with a stamped,
addressed envelope suitable for its return. (See *Writing
for the BBC*, BBC Publications.)

Criticism

1 Choose one of the scripts. At which points in it would
the writer expect the studio audience to laugh?

2 With the help of *Radio Times* and *TV Times*, make a
list of situation comedies transmitted on the various
television channels over the course of a month. What
are their recurring subjects and themes?

3 Select one of the scripts in this collection. Imagine
you are directing it for television. What studio
settings would you need? Would filming on location
be necessary? What characteristics will you be
looking for in the actors and actresses who might
play the minor roles?

4   Do you like a situation comedy to be realistic? Which of the shows in this book do you find most authentic or true-to-life? Which do you like best? Why?

5   Do you consider any of these scripts (or individual jokes) to be in 'bad taste'? Which current series on television, if any, do you think might be offensive to some viewers?

6   Collect together a number of reviews of a comedy show you have seen recently. Which do you think are fair? Try reviewing another show (or one of the scripts in this book).

7   Some newspapers 'preview' forthcoming programmes. With the help of *Radio Times* and *TV Times*, try writing a preview of a forthcoming comedy programme, making your own judgements on whether you would recommend the show to other viewers.

8   To what extent do you accept the points made in the articles from the *BBC Handbook* and *ITV Yearbook* quoted in the introduction?